Magical F...

Homes & Gardens

BARBARA PURCHIA AND E. ASHLEY ROONEY
FOREWORD BY DAVID D. J. RAU

SCHIFFER PUBLISHING

4880 Lower Valley Road • Atglen, PA 19310

T0267193

Cover design by Ashley Millhouse
Images courtesy of the artist, unless otherwise noted.
Front cover and page 1: Andrea Riggillo-Masia / photographer Caryn McCowan; back cover: Madeline Kwasniewski; left flap: Jessica Zeedyk; spine: John Curtis Crawford
Chapter start images courtesy of Bigstock: Tiny cute fairy cottages in a magical forest, copyright © youmotion; Purple passionflower called Passiflora incarnate blooms on a post with a fairy garden mason jar light glowing in Sarasota, Florida, copyright © Rose911; Deep in a distant, hidden, mysterious forest sits an enchanting fairy tree home inside an old white oak, copyright © ratpack2; Deep in a distant, hidden, mysterious forest sits an enchanting fairy tree home, copyright © MaaraMore; Digital illustration fairy tree house in fantasy forest with stone road copyright © MaaraMore; Deep in a distant, hidden, mysterious forest sits an enchanting fairy tree home inside an old white oak, copyright © MaaraMore.

Type set in Korinna BT/Fairplex Wide & Narrow/Baskerville Display PT

Authors' note: For consistency, we have used the modern spelling of "fairy" instead of "faerie" except where specified by the artist.

ISBN: 978-0-7643-6745-8
Printed in China

Published by Schiffer Publishing, Ltd.
4880 Lower Valley Road
Atglen, PA 19310
Phone: (610) 593-1777; Fax: (610) 593-2002
Email: info@schifferbooks.com
Web: www.schifferbooks.com

For our complete selection of fine books on this and related subjects, please visit our website at www.schifferbooks.com. You may also write for a free catalog.

Schiffer Publishing's titles are available at special discounts for bulk purchases for sales promotions or premiums. Special editions, including personalized covers, corporate imprints, and excerpts, can be created in large quantities for special needs. For more information, contact the publisher.

Other Schiffer Books by the Authors:
Fairy Homes and Gardens, 978-0-7643-4698-9
Glass Art: 112 Contemporary Artists, 978-0-7643-5188-4
Contemporary Sand Sculpture, 978-0-7643-5474-8
Contemporary Ice Sculpture, 978-0-7643-5641-4

FSC
www.fsc.org
MIX
Paper from responsible sources
FSC® C167893

Contents

FOREWORD
04

INTRODUCTION
20

— 1 —   FAIRY COMMUNITIES   24

— 2 —   COTTAGES   64

— 3 —   FAIRY HOUSES   92

— 4 —   CASTLES, CHALETS, AND OTHER
         SERENDIPITOUS STRUCTURES   106

— 5 —   FAIRY ACCESSORIES   120

— 6 —   THE DESIGNERS   132

APPENDIX:
PLANTS FOR YOUR FAIRY GARDEN
142

Foreword

FAIRIES AT THE MUSEUM:
THE STORY OF THE WEE FAERIE VILLAGE AT FLORENCE
GRISWOLD MUSEUM IN OLD LYME, CONNECTICUT

by David D. J. Rau

A girl dressed as a green fairy tours through Wee Faerie
Village in the Land of Oz, 2013. *Photograph by Sean Flynn*

Tinkle-Tink! Tinkle-Tink!

A ring-jingle is a simple bracelet of sorts created with two shiny beads, a small jingle bell, and a length of elastic. The jingle bell's "tinkle-tink" sound warns of a human's arrival, so the fairies can quickly flutter away. Hundreds of the shiny homemade baubles hung silently on jewelry racks ready for the opening day of the very first Lyme Art Colony's Wee Faerie Village.

It was a picture-perfect October Saturday at the museum in 2009. The trees on the property were still mostly green, but tinges of orange and yellow hinted at the riotous beauty to come. Morning light danced on waves of the river's incoming tide, and the late-blooming pink and white Sheffield mums swayed in the gardens beside the barns. The campus was abuzz with anticipation.

Griswold Boardinghouse in fall

Shortly before 10 a.m., the first car pulled into the driveway. Soon, a caravan of cars quickly filled up the first parking lot, then the second, and then the third. Excited visitors—some wearing fairy wings, pink and purple tutus, and sparkly tiaras—filled the lobby to capacity. Gleeful chatter rose to a deafening din. The ticket line spilled from the lobby out the front door and up the sidewalk for the first time in the museum's history. It was a wee-fairy blockbuster.

Out of necessity, the museum staff moved faster and faster, and then faster still. Additional staff and volunteers were called in. The bounty of ring-jingles that had filled the counters that morning diminished as visitors of all ages wriggled them onto their wrists, grabbed their keepsake maps, and set off in search of fairies. As the day continued, the families just kept coming. It seemed to be a grand success.

However, not all that glitters is golden fairy dust. In a matter of hours, trash cans were overloaded, restrooms were messy, and a well-trodden path was forming along the perimeter of the campus. The fairy stock in the shop was growing woefully low, the carpet was teeming with glitter, and the stock of ring-jingles dwindled to single digits. It was time to better prepare for the three weeks of fairy village that lay ahead. The museum was committed to this enchanted experiment. Parking attendants would be hired, portable toilets rented,

Along the river with a shady tree, 2009. *Photograph by Sean Flynn*

cleaning teams assembled, and jingle bells shipped overnight. Happy from a day of exhilarating work, the staff headed home, each with a bag filled with beads, bells, and elastic—the essential ring-jingle-making materials—to prepare for the second day of the event—which, we now know, was busier still. Tinkle-tink. Tinkle-tink. Tinkle-tink.

Miss Florence and the Artists of Old Lyme

The museum's namesake, Florence Griswold, was the youngest daughter of Robert Harper Griswold, a New England sea captain who sailed packet boats transporting people and parcels from New York to London and back. Indeed, *Moby Dick* author Herman Melville was a passenger on one of these weeks-long voyages across the Atlantic. The young captain's esteemed position with the shipping company afforded him the means to purchase one of the finest homes on Lyme Street in the bucolic village of Old Lyme. Sadly, the captain was away at sea when Florence Ann Griswold was born on Christmas Day in 1850.

Florence never married or had any children; by 1899, she was quite alone in the world. Her brother Robbie died of illness, and her sister Louise was killed in a carriage accident. Her only remaining sister, Adele, needed to be institutionalized in Hartford for unknown reasons. With her parents gone, Florence was the sole resident of the Griswold House. To earn a living, she continued the family's practice of renting out rooms to travelers and locals in need of a place to stay.

One such traveler was Henry Ward Ranger, an artist from New York City scouting a location for his dream of starting an American artist colony. He needed a place for his fellow artists to stay, surrounded by interesting subject matter to be painted and hosted by a sympathetic patron who would not mind a bevy of bohemian painters invading her genteel way of life. On a fateful summer day, he found all of this at Miss Florence's.

Ranger returned the following summer with a merry band of artists and filled Miss Florence's boardinghouse from the first floor to the attic. The artists painted *en plein air*, or out-of-doors, all day and gathered for meals in the dining room or on the side porch. They spent their evenings entertaining one another in the parlor with music, games, and artistic challenges. With Miss Florence's permission, they began the practice of painting pictures on the doors, depicting scenes such as moonlit landscapes or resting cows, which looked like scenes through a window. When doors became scarce, the artists began to paint on wooden panels of various sizes and installed them on the dining-room walls, creating

an intimate yet dazzling picture gallery. The house was once again filled with life, noise, and art—and also many, many cats.

Over the next decade or so, the artists kept coming to Old Lyme to paint. Childe Hassam (1859–1935) was one of the most famous painters to visit Miss Florence's, and he brought with him to the Lyme Art Colony an American version of impressionism. Inspired by painters such as Claude Monet and Auguste Renoir, the American artists captured light-filled Connecticut scenes on their canvases and wooden panels, painted in bright colors with loose and obvious brushstrokes. They painted white New England churches, farm fields framed with stone walls, and sunny, flower-filled gardens. Eventually, Miss Florence's ebullient boardinghouse for artists became known far and wide as the "home of American impressionism." Her hospitality was legendary, and she became lifelong friends with many artists whose careers blossomed under her care.

Miss Florence died in 1937, surrounded by a pair of painters and her two favorite cats. The house became a local history museum open to the public after the Second World War. By then, most of the land had been sold, as well as the contents of the house. However, the painted doors and panels remained in place. After years of reclaiming the surrounding land and Miss Florence's effects, the museum today occupies the original 12 acres of gardens and grounds along the Lieutenant River, complete with the historic house, a state-of-the-art gallery, an education center, a landscape center, and a historic artist studio. By 2002, when the new gallery was completed, nearly 40,000 visitors came annually. They came to see the historic house and learn the story of Miss Florence and the artists of Old Lyme. They came to tour the changing exhibitions of art in

Opposite page
Left: Childe Hassam painting *Apple Trees in Bloom*, Old Lyme, 1904. Lyme Historical Society Archives at the Florence Griswold Museum. *Photograph courtesy of Florence Griswold Museum*

Right: John R. Baynes, *Hot Air Club*, 1905, Lyme Historical Society Archives at the Florence Griswold Museum. *Photograph courtesy of Florence Griswold Museum*

the gallery. They came to walk the restored flower and vegetable gardens. It was all very peaceful, orderly, and predictable. Then, in 2009, the fairies arrived, and the museum would never be the same.

THE CHALLENGE_____
The Wee Faerie Village

It all began with a simple challenge. What could the museum do with minimal money for a big impact? The financial crisis of 2008 convinced similar cultural institutions to hunker down and wait for better days. The Florence Griswold Museum, however, decided to go big—by going very small—and presented the very first Wee Faerie Village for three weeks in October 2009.

Inspired by the popularity of fairy events elsewhere, such as an annual celebration in Portsmouth, New Hampshire, the idea to install fairy houses in the museum gardens was born. But where to begin? The greatest challenge was to align the fun and fanciful event with the museum's mission to educate the public on the art and history of Connecticut, with an emphasis on the Lyme Art Colony. Where does fairy glitter fit in? It seemed only natural that the museum's first fairy village would be inspired by the historic art colony. The resident fairies were imagined as the creative muses for the original artists, and their enchanting dwellings each would reference a specific artist in clever and creative ways.

The first step was to find artists who could create the various fairy installations for free. A few years earlier, the museum had launched *Miss Florence's Artist Trees* by inviting artists to paint in their signature style on blank palettes to be hung as ornaments on Christmas trees during the museum's annual celebration. The goal the first year was to enlist fifty local artists, which became the initial list of possible Wee Faerie Village artists. Over forty artists participated in the fairy village during the first year—and almost none of them had any previous experience working on similar projects. To provide sage advice on this new realm, the museum reached out to Tracy Kane, noted fairy author and co-organizer of the Portsmouth event, who eagerly joined the

Griswold the Boy Faerie. Illustrated by Jeffrey Himmelman, 2009

Florence the Girl Faerie. Illustrated by Jeffrey Himmelman, 2009

creative team. Fairy books and magazines were ordered. It was all starting to come together, acorn by acorn, feather by feather.

As preparations continued, it became clear that the museum would need to create a map for visitors to find the fairy installations on campus. A local author and illustrator recommended his son, Jeffrey Himmelman, a recent graduate from the School for the Visual Arts in New York, who was working on fantasy imagery in the world of computer gaming. His first task was to help give the project an identity, and for that he created a pair of fairy mascots, cleverly named Griswold and Florence.

Griswold's fairy wings resemble oak leaves and maple seedlings. He is clad in clothes of tight-fitting leaves and wears an acorn cap beret. The impish Griswold is the essence of creativity, holding a scroll of drawing paper in one hand and a spear-like ink pen in the other. In contrast, Florence is sweet and demure. She grasps a human-scale paintbrush, and her painter's palette and tiny jars of pigment are fastened to her belt. Her leafy ensemble is completed with a crown of purple flowers. The duo was the perfect depiction of what the Lyme Art Colony artists' fairy muses might look like.

Along with the map, the museum produced a cell phone tour (a novel notion at the time) to explain how each fairy's homestead connected to his or her historic artist. The short scripts were performed by the local high school's theater department. It was decided that the fairies would not be physically depicted in the installations; instead, visitors would discover clues that each fairy had just been there working in the garden, painting a picture, or cooking dinner. This illusion that the fairies just fluttered away when they heard the tinkle of the ring-jingles made the homes seem alive and active rather than static and sculptural.

What the artists produced that first year was remarkable. For example, to capture the creative spirit of Childe Hassam, who often painted pictures of the Old Lyme Congregational Church, Tracy Kane fashioned a church-like dwelling out of a stump with a pointy limb. The steeple clock was made out of a sand dollar and seeds. Another artist captured Matilda Browne's love of painting flowers by crafting a

Connecticut saltbox out of a used pastel box shingled with pumpkin seeds, the ridge of the roof lined with acorn caps. One of the real artistic challenges was longevity. The installations made of feathers, twigs, moss, and seeds needed to be weather resistant to look presentable for three weeks. October weather in Connecticut can be glorious, but the fairy villages over the last decade have experienced wind, rain, heavy sudden snowfalls—and even a hurricane!

During the first Wee Faerie Village, the museum welcomed over 10,000 visitors—about a quarter of the museum's annual attendance in three weeks' time. The museum hosted weekly craft sessions for families, which proved very popular and provided

visitors young and old with materials and instruction to create fairy wands and crowns. The air of the education center shimmered with glitter.

The museum quality of the fairy installations excited visitors and inspired many to create as well. Tracy Kane had advised that many families enjoy making fairy houses on-site at other fairy events; with this in mind, the museum identified a small woodland section of the property as "Beyond the Beyond" and encouraged visitors to make their own fairy dwellings with materials found on the forest floor. After the first weekend, the woodland area was brimming with creative constructions. Sticks were jabbed in the ground, neatly aligned; colored

Top left: *Charter Oak Estates* by Barbara Stevens and Barbara O'Connell, 2009. *Photograph by Sean Flynn*

Left: *Water Fall Downs* by Craig Nelson, 2009. *Photograph by Sean Flynn*

Top right: *Water Water Everywhere* by Tracy Kane, 2009. *Photograph by Sean Flynn*

leaves were arranged in patterns; and tree bark was delicately balanced—all for the goal of creating wee fairy shelters. Museum staff left all the visitors' dwellings as they were, only to discover that the next day's visitors would repurpose the materials from the houses to construct their own. For three weeks, this makeshift community transformed daily. The keepsake map encouraged families to keep the fairy magic going at home by creating a fairy house in their yard or garden and sending pictures to the museum. Many did.

The Fairies Take a Hiatus ... and Make a Triumphant Return

Throughout the run of the first fairy village, visitors continually inquired if the museum was planning to make the fairies an annual event. Back then,

Riverbend Way by Robb Nestor and Bill Reynolds, 2009. *Photograph by Sean Flynn*

the short answer was simply "No." In theory, the museum was testing the public's reaction to a creative October event on the grounds, the first of which was the Wee Faerie Village. Prior to the fairies, the museum had always seen a lull in attendance after the busy summer tourist season, despite the popularity of foliage season in New England. October is a naturally stunning month as the museum grounds go from green to gold over the course of the four weeks. The museum was curious to learn if other outdoor creative endeavors could also be popular.

With that in mind, the following October the museum presented *Scarecrows at the Museum*, which featured scarecrows based on Vincent van Gogh, Jackson Pollock, Frida Kahlo, Marc Chagall, Piet Mondrian, and other famous artists. A year later, the museum presented *Of Feathers and Fairy Tales: Birdhouses at the Museum*, for which artists chose a classic tale and fashioned a fantastical birdhouse home based on the story. Both the scarecrows and the birdhouses were popular, but neither event approached the popularity of the fairies.

During the fourth October, the museum returned to the fairy realm. Not wanting to repeat the art colony theme of the first year, the museum opted to highlight the subject matter that inspired the Lyme painters. For *Wee Faerie Village in the Land of Picture Making*, fairy dwellings were based on the trees, the marsh, the flowers, and the dazzling sunlight on the river. A map for visitors offered short descriptions of each dwelling, with the popular "Can you find me?" object hidden in each one. The return to the fairy theme was met with a robust attendance that overtook the previous two years. It was clear that the museum would be smart to focus on fairies each October.

With Wee Faerie Village as the main theme, the new challenge was to come up with an alluring theme each year to keep the event fresh for visitors and to inspire the talented Wee Faerie Village artists. To emphasize the changing theme, the museum commissioned Aaron B. Miller of Chicago, on the basis of a recommendation by Jeffrey Himmelman (whose gaming career was skyrocketing), to supply yearly artwork and assistance with the fairy map. Each year to follow, Miller would create a half-dozen fairy characters that helped visually define that year's themes. Since that first Saturday in October 2009, over 130,500 visitors have ventured to Old Lyme to explore the Wee Faerie Village and other creative October endeavors. Clearly, the fairies' enchanting powers to ignite the imagination of the young and the young at heart are stronger than ever. The book you are holding is proof of this. Here's to the twinkle, the glimmer, and the glow that the fairy realm continues to spark in all of us.

David D. J. Rau is the director of education and outreach at the Florence Griswold Museum and for the last decade has been an artist and impresario for the museum's outdoor Wee Faerie Village events. When not crafting fairy houses, Rau works in his home studio to create intricate assemblages often incorporating vintage items, miniature furniture, and lush materials.

Airborne Cottages by Tracy Kane, 2012.
Photograph by Sean Flynn

Nevergreen Caverns by David D. J. Rau, 2012.
Photograph by Sean Flynn

River Valley Farm by Sandra Bender Fromson, 2012. *Photograph by Sean Flynn*

Opposite page
Top: *Water Pearl Palace* by Dylan and Ted Gaffney, 2012. *Photograph by Sean Flynn*

Bottom: *Sakuyu, a Japanese Faerie Garden* by Garden Gang members Bobbie Padgett, DeeDee Charnock, Gay Thorn, Teddi Curtiss, and Sheila Wertheimer, 2012. *Photograph by Sean Flynn*

Mihashirano's Tea House by Anita Walsh, 2012. Photograph by Sean Flynn

Inset: *The Wee Faerie Finder*. Illustrated by *Jeffrey Himmelman, 2012*

Wee Faerie Village in the Land of Oz (2013)

Frank L. Baum's children's story, *The Wonderful Wizard of Oz* was first published in 1900, the first year of the Lyme Art Colony. To honor the coincidence, the fairy artists retold the story of Dorothy traveling to Oz in twenty-four installations. The museum also commissioned the Flock Theater of New London, Connecticut, to present nighttime tours combining Miss Florence and the Oz story, turning the historic house into a shadow-puppet theater. This was the most popular Wee Faerie Village to date, attracting more than 17,000 visitors in one month.

Wee Faerie Village in a Steampunk'd Wonderland (2014)

To give a modern twist to Lewis Carroll's classic Victorian story *Alice in Wonderland*, fairy artists incorporated motifs from the popular Steampunk movement, inspired by science fiction stories set in the steam-powered past.

Whimsical Kingdoms: Legendary Castles, Towers, and Palaces (2015)

Fairy artists each picked a story featuring either a castle (*Cinderella*), a tower (*Rapunzel*), or a palace (*Aladdin*) and created a fairy-scale version of the setting. This event featured thirty-two fictional fortifications by more than fifty artists and hundreds of talented elementary school artists. The museum commissioned sand sculptor Greg J. Grady Jr. to transform 8,000 pounds of flat-grain sand into the ultimate sandcastle, and chain-saw artist Jared Welcome transformed a storm-damaged sugar maple into an enchanted castle.

A Flutter in Time: Faerie Houses Around the World & Across the Ages (2016)

Fairy artists envisioned how and where fairies have been living since the dawn of time, conjuring up remarkable dwellings inspired by architecture found around the world and beyond—from Giza, Egypt, in 2500 BCE to outer space in 2817.

Faerieville, U.S.A.: In and Around a Wee Faerie Town (2017)

Focusing on small-town America, the Wee Faerie Village became a veritable village of wee fairies going about their busy day, with thirty-one installations including a bakery, a farmers' market, a schoolhouse, a church, a factory, a bookstore, a flower shop, a train depot, and a drive-in movie theater.

Lettersburg Junction: Wee Faerie Homesteads from A to Z and 1-2-3 (2018)

Each fairy artist or team chose a letter or symbol and built a fairy house to match. Often, the letter was the inspiration for the shape of the structure, as well as many of the contents.

Supertopia: Superheroes' Headquarters and Hideaways (2019)

Fairy artists chose famous, infamous, or lesser-known superheroes or villains and built fairy versions of their headquarters or hideaways. For the first year, the fairy map route took advantage of the museum's newly installed Artists' Trail, a series of recently planted pathways circumnavigating the riverside campus.

Folly Woods: Awesome Wee Faerie Architecture along the Artists' Trail (2021—postponed from October 2020 due to COVID-19)

Architectural follies are traditionally whimsical structures designed to enhance picturesque scenes at grand estates and public parks. Fairy artists constructed miniature architectural marvels—archways, temples, pavilions, and such—set along the Artists' Trail.

Twinkle Point: An Amusement Park for the Wee Faerie Folk (2022)

Shrieks, whoops, and giggles filled the air at Twinkle Point, an amusement park perfectly sized for the wee fairies. Fairy artists created miniature theme park rides such as rollercoasters, merry-go-rounds, and fun houses

Fathom Heights: A Sea Faerie Civilization (2023)

Fathom Heights was a fashionable underwater world where the wee sea fairies—the magical creatures sporting both wings and fins—live, work, and play. The "underwater" village was filled with sea fairies' houses as well as a botanical garden, an art museum, a zoo, and more.

Left column, top to bottom:

Visitor in character in Poppy Field, 2013. *Photograph by Sean Flynn*

The Cowardly Lion by Diana DeWolf-Carfi and Skylar Carfi, 2013. *Photograph by Sean Flynn*

Detail of *The Council with the Munchkins* by members of the museum's Garden Gang: Dee Charnok, Teddi Curtiss, Bobbie Padgett, and Gay Thorne, 2013. *Photograph by Sean Flynn*

Right column, top to bottom:

Detail of *Queen of Heart Castle* by Megan Jeffery, 2014. *Photograph by Sean Flynn*

A Garden of Talking Flowers by Julie Solz and Steve Hansen, 2014. *Photograph by Sean Flynn*

Opposite page, clockwise from top left

Sandcastle by Greg J. Grady Jr., 2015. *Photograph by Sean Flynn*; *Mesa Verde, Colorado (circa 615)* by Carol Hall-Jordan and Kathryn Stocking-Koza, 2016. *Photograph by Sean Flynn*; *All Pro Automotive of Faerieville* by Dave Graybill, 2017. *Photograph by Sean Flynn*; *Faerieville Hardware Co.* by Lori and Rich Lenz, 2017. *Photograph by Cheryl Poirier*; *Faerieville Depot* by Linda Turner and Gerry Urbanik, 2017. *Photograph by Sean Flynn*; *One Thousand and One Arabian Nights* by Pam Erickson and Sharon Didato, 2015. *Photograph by Sean Flynn*

Millie's Sweets & Treats by Lisa Kenyon and Michael, Lily, and Elizabeth Harney, 2022. *Photograph courtesy of the Florence Griswold Museum*

The Busy Bee Tailoring Buzziness by Zenaida Davis, Pam Erickson, and Anna Lindquist, 2019. *Photograph by Sean Flynn*

Bat Faerie's Batcave by David D. J. Rau, 2019. *Photograph by Sean Flynn*

Faerie Thor's Viking Realm by Lori and Rich Lenz, 2019. *Photograph by Sean Flynn*

Opposite page
Top left: *Rain Barrel Retreat* by Julie Solz and Steve Hansen, 2018. *Photograph by Sean Flynn*

Inset: *M Is for Mini Manor* by Megan Jeffery, 2018. *Photograph by Sean Flynn*

Fairy: *Morning Glory. Illustrated by Aaron B. Miller, 2019*

Bottom: *S Is for Shadyside Stitchery* by Pam Erickson, 2018. *Photograph by Sean Flynn*

Above
Left: *Iron Faerie's Stark Tower Faerie Complex* by Kristen Thornton, 2019. *Photograph by Sean Flynn*

Right: *Captain America's Lighthouse* by Steve Rodgers, 2019. *Photograph by Sean Flynn*

Introduction

In the image: "My Happy Place", "Be Kind", "Be Bold", "Be thankful", "Enjoy the ride", "Come Shine with Us"

DESPITE ALL OUR MODERN TECHNOLOGY, FAIRIES CONTINUE TO INSPIRE US!

Jessica Marro appeals to our senses with this humble bark-covered cottage.

Fairies live in the realm between reality and imagination, fascination and enchantment. They come and go as they please, most often without being seen. They like people, especially children and kind, generous grown-ups. They like colorful flowers, aromatic herbs, and mossy floors. Sprinkle fairy dust and shiny objects to attract them. People like fairy houses and gardens because they emphasize being one with nature, using our imagination, and reusing things. We can help fairies by creating a place for them to live, work, sleep, and dream.

Designing, creating, and maintaining a fairy home and garden can be a personal challenge, a family activity, an educational tool, or even a form of meditation. It doesn't have to be completed all at once. We can begin it and then step away for some time only to return later and work toward our vision. Some of us find joy in the process; some enjoy the pride of the finished product. With the hectic pace of modern life, setting aside time for ourselves to relax and be creative is no longer a luxury—it's essential for our health.

To make a fairy house, we can go outside to explore the woods, the seashore, and the park down the street. We can make swings from milkweed pods, houses from pumpkin or coconut shells, bowls from acorn tops, and beds from dried rose petals and dried English ivy leaves. We can forage for fairy material in our jewelry box and at tag sales and flea markets, and we can go through those small or miniature toys that have been outgrown. We can use thimbles as vases, fishing flies as flowers, buttons as plates or tabletops, empty spools for chairs or tables, paper baking cups or scraps of cloth as tablecloths, and beads for door knockers or the balustrades of balconies. Christmas tree decorations are an easy source of supplies. Some call this upcycling or "creative reuse," which is the process of transforming useless or unwanted items into new materials or products thought to have greater artistic or environmental value. Yes, of course, you can purchase fairy garden accessories, which may help inspire you too.

It's an easy step from listening to a fairy tale to building a fairy house. Unlike dollhouses, where objects are made to look like tiny versions of the

Fairy Bell House by Steve Rodgers. The Bell Fairy sounds the alarm to alert all the other fairies in the forest of looming dangers.

Willow the Wise Fairy by Andrea Riggillo-Masia. The walls are covered with delicate bark paper from a twisted oak. Birchwood is used for the bed, shelf, and chair. A recycled earring becomes a hanging ornament, acorns become candleholders, and shells become bookends. *Courtesy of Caryn McCowan*

real thing, fairy houses incorporate another level of imagination, transforming natural objects such as an old tree stump into new homes for the spirits. Or perhaps you want to build something entirely new. You can add moss to look like grass, twigs to look like miniature trees, and pebbles to look like boulders. Designers often let the materials decide where they want to be and how they want to be combined. Perhaps a designer will start with a large seashell, an old teapot, or a broken planter and add twigs, bark, flowers, rocks, shells, pods, herbs, or succulents.

Designers may festoon an old birdcage as a perfect fairy hideaway and add dried flowers as a work of art to be hung on the fairy's wall. Pine cone scales or tree fungi can be used as roofing elements. Imagine a colorful leaf as a snuggly blanket. Little bits of cloth, buttons, marbles, beads, or jewelry (you know that one earring for which you can't find the matching one) can be used to decorate or enhance a fairy dwelling. Almost anything can be something else with a little imagination and some manipulation.

For a charming fairy house, all you need is imagination. You can place it anywhere: on your dining-room table, up against a big tree, or in the garden. You can cover the ground with blue star creeper, moss, sedum, bark bits, or creeping thyme to form a tiny green carpet. You can use small plants as tiny, growing elements. You can add a pool or wishing well. By letting the fairy world know that you support nature, you can show the fairies you understand and value the same things they do.

In the foreword, David D. J. Rau recalled how fairy houses kept the Florence Griswold Museum alive in more ways than one. On the following pages, more than twenty designers show us their creations, with some offering tips on how they made their designs and sharing stories about how fairies live in their homes. Unless otherwise noted, all photographs were taken by their fairy house designers. In the appendix, we suggest plants for fairy homes for both inside and outside. You may want to keep your fairy house outside in the warmer weather and bring it inside when it gets cooler.

Cedar Hollow Place by Pamela Godsoe. Some fairies move to warmer climates during the winter, but this home's residents stay year-round. *Courtesy of Katrina McCaul / @moseymeadow*

Here, a fairy village surrounds the tree. *Photograph by Elyse Purchia*

Readers can use this book to admire the creativity of these designers and get inspiration for building a fairy house. The fairy houses here are built in communities, as castles, houses, and cottages. They are built for special events and to tell stories and because, yes, we do believe in fairies!

Mihashirano's Tea House by Anita Walsh. Mihashirano, the fairy goddess of green-growing things, works hard alongside her mom, Amaterasu, the Sun Goddess, to help things grow along the river. The location for Mihashirano's tea house was chosen by a bird. Can you find this mystical bird and Mihashirano's sailboat? *Photograph by Sean Flynn*

This fairy home by Kathleen Nolan was hidden in a tree as part of the Plymouth Fairy Door Trail in Massachusetts.

— 1 —
Fairy Communities

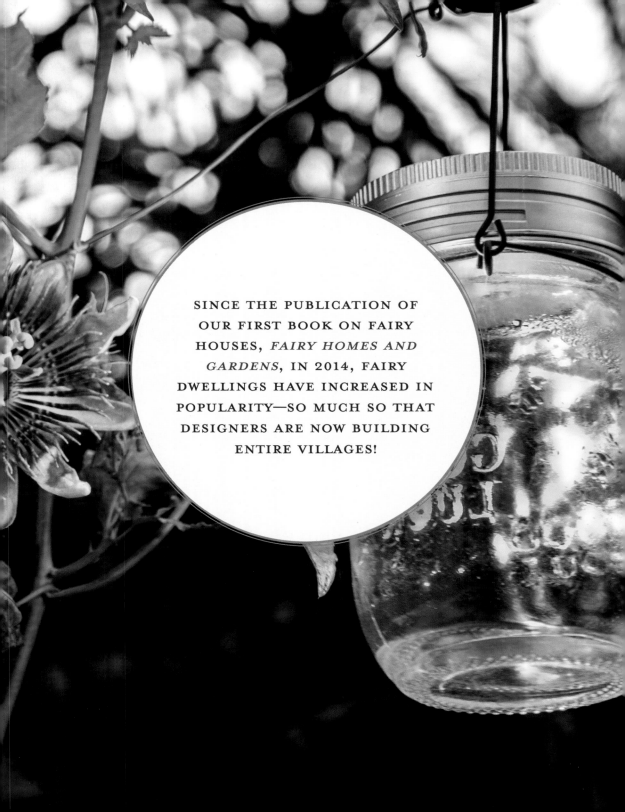

SINCE THE PUBLICATION OF
OUR FIRST BOOK ON FAIRY
HOUSES, *FAIRY HOMES AND
GARDENS*, IN 2014, FAIRY
DWELLINGS HAVE INCREASED IN
POPULARITY—SO MUCH SO THAT
DESIGNERS ARE NOW BUILDING
ENTIRE VILLAGES!

Ariel's Aviary

IN AN ABANDONED AVIARY, ARIEL AND HER FAIRY FRIENDS
ARE BUILDING A BRAND-NEW WORLD THAT CELEBRATES
KINDESS TOWARD THE ENVIRONMENT AND OTHER BEINGS.

Installed view of *Ariel's Aviary* on the Florence Griswold
Museum campus. The central folly is the dome-shaped aviary
containing the hatchling (i.e., the gazing ball). *Courtesy of
William Evertson*

Sometime after the 2020 global pandemic, Ariel and her fairy friends found a new-world hatchling in an abandoned aviary. The fairies understood the importance of their discovery and the opportunity it presented to create a brand-new world where humans will have a second chance to be kinder to the environment and each other. Although the aviary is beautiful, it doesn't offer much protection for the hatchling. The fairies built their homes in a circle around the hatchling and vowed to do their part to protect the new emerging world. Look into the gazing ball. Can you see the key to a kinder new world?

On the following pages, you will find a forest infirmary, museum, recycling center, library, bandstand, vineyard, and community center in addition to the main aviary created by the Original Art Party, a group of creatives consisting of William and Ian Evertson, Teri and Flip Prestash, Cynthia and Roger Abraham, Nancy and Lance Crouch, and Nancy and Jed Dolde.

The community center combines wood slabs, pine cones, moss, slate, and other natural materials. Paper origami cranes are also visible as a reference both to the aviary and the peace cranes of Hiroshima. *Courtesy of William Evertson*

The library steps are created from decommissioned books. Small painted twigs fill the shelves, and a grass-thatched roof completes the building. *Courtesy of Cynthia Abraham*

Top left: Fairies are keen on music as a vital part of the transition to a kinder, gentler postpandemic world. The Beatle Bandstand is constructed of a clay pot, acorn caps, and moss. *Courtesy of Cynthia Abraham*

Top right: The forest infirmary takes shape from a tangle of branches and provides the fairies a space to plant and tend to the endangered forests. *Courtesy of Cynthia Abraham*

Left: In the Mushroom Museum, the mushrooms act as galleries featuring many famous fairy artists eager to inspire a kinder world. The mushrooms are constructed of wire, wire mesh, and painted thin-set adhesive mortar. *Courtesy of Teri Prestash*

Hidden Village of Pachysandra

ONCE UPON A TIME . . .

there was a little girl named Andrea Riggillo-Masia who pulled her bright-red wagon to the library and filled it with giant volumes of fairy tales by the Brothers Grimm, Hans Christian Andersen, and Lewis Carroll. Andrea loved the magical stories so much she would sleep with her books and daydream of a fairy godmother, a handsome prince, and happily ever after. Then she grew up. Now she creates fairy homes and villages.

Built of curling natural birch and oak bark with acorn towers, this village contains fairy life within each house. Handmade birch furniture and recycled adornments are built and used. Most roofs lift up to show the top floor.

Photographs courtesy of Caryn McCowan

Moved by Romanian music and folklore of gypsies, the tarot, and wanderlust, Andrea built the Travelin' Fairy of Tarot for her village.

The gypsy caravan is hand-built of wood. Cork and moss cover the exterior.

Inside, a candlelit gypsy's table is set up for tarot card reading or crystal ball gazing. In an alcove, there is a cove bed and Indie credenza.

Andrea's fairy village has homes that range from 7 to 14 inches tall. It includes the Toast and Tea Tavern with its acorn tower, Uldred the Gnome's home, and Dew Drop Fairy Sisters at Birchwood Forest.

Dew Drop Fairy Sisters at Birchwood Forest was inspired by Beltane, the Gaelic May Day festival, springtime, clean water, and sunshine. Birch bark from her own trees and fresh eucalyptus leaves adorn this reconstructed birdhouse with a waterwheel and tiny slide for the fairy bunny. Inside there is a tiny pool of water and more. Built of wood, curling natural birch bark, and oak bark, each abode holds a thematic fairy's life within.

Inset: This 10-inch-tall fairy chamber was created for the old crone Baba Yaga. It has pine cone shingles with twisted twigs on the moss roof, and inside a hearth has bedding on top to keep warm in winter! This is a windup musical piece.

Fairy Houses in Cappadocia

When invited to participate in Florence Griswold Museum's 2016 exhibit, *A Flutter in Time: Faerie Houses Around the World & Across the Ages*, Nancy MacBride chose Cappadocia, a semiarid region in central Turkey known for its distinctive "fairy chimneys"—tall, cone-shaped rock formations—and other natural wonders. Cappadocia villagers carve out houses, churches, and monasteries from the soft rocks of volcanic deposits.

Modern Turkish people live in comfortable cave homes, and tourists can even find a hotel room in these carved-out communities. Fairies love to use natural materials to build their homes, so, of course, they would be inspired by these Turkish homes.

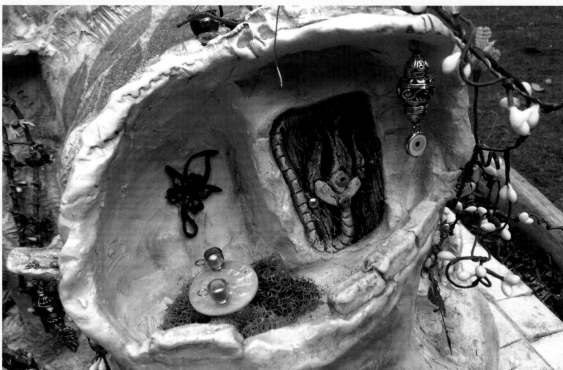

Top left: This fairy house is mostly ceramic.

Top center: The carvings on the doors are inspired by traditional Turkish designs, including the Turkish tulip.

Top right: Firewood is gathered, and the fairies have just started a fire under the pot to warm up some nectar.

The Nazars (or blue eyes) are traditional ancient amulets that repel evil to keep the residents of the home safe. A large mother-of-pearl button is employed as a tabletop on the balcony.

Shoots and Ladders

When they were children, Madeline Kwasniewski and her siblings would spend the night at their grandparents' house. They loved playing Chutes and Ladders. So, one day when walking through her garden, Madeleine envisioned little fairies playing in her garden, climbing little ladders and sliding down her flower shoots!

Madeline created a charming three-house village to reflect her favorite childhood games and memories.

Miss Daisy's house is 8 by 16 inches. Hand-cut 100-year-old cedar shingles compose the roof, mushrooms are the awnings, Popsicle sticks are the shutters, and branch twigs form the arbor. There's a touch of silk flowers and dashes of yellow acrylic paint, and the birdbath is a green flat rock with a beach shell. Dried, painted weeds are the background. A little fox is always present in Madeline's displays.

Thistle Do is 6 by 7 inches. The cedar shingles are hand-cut, the roof trim is cut pine cones, and the door is made of found wood trimmed with cloves. There is a driftwood tree, a dried seedpod for a hammock, a touch of silk flowers, and a dash of lavender acrylic paint. The fox is nearby keeping an eye out for the fairies.

For-Get-Me-Knot is 6 by 7 inches. The roof is hand-cut 100-year-old cedar, trimmed with cut pine cones. The door is found wood trimmed with cloves. Pine cone bushes are on the side of the house, and the fountain is made from mussel shells. The bird feeder is wood with mustard seeds; there is a touch of silk flowers and a dash of blue acrylic paint.

Polynesian Paradise

Created by Jessica Zeedyk, *Polynesian Paradise* was a part of the themed exhibit *A Flutter in Time: Faerie Houses Around the World & Across the Ages* in Wee Faerie Village at the Florence Griswold Museum in 2016. The open-air huts are of various sizes and mediums. The main structures are made from wood, bamboo, grass, and ribbon woven from banana leaves.

This display sat in a raised garden bed nestled in various flower plants and greens local to New England. To add a bit of the tropics, Jessica used a few man-made *Monstera* plant leaves and palm fronds. Most of this village is filled with natural elements of shells, sand, moss, and driftwood. The durable blue vinyl gives the appearance of a beautiful blue ocean and withstands the elements. The wooden outrigger canoe is 10 inches long.

The village kitchen is the largest of the structures in the village. Sitting on stilts, it measures 20 inches from floor to roof's peak. The shells on the side are made to look as if they are catching the rain. The flowing water is made from a mixture of hot glue and a resin. The lighting fixture is a mix of glass beads affixed to a bamboo frame.

The semienclosed meeting house has banana leaf woven walls and bamboo structural supports. On each side of the opening, attached to carved wooden beads, are torches made from orange glass beads to look as if they are lit with a flame. The exterior is also adorned with shell leis, moss, and the same arched bamboo entrance found on each of the structures in the village. Inside the meetinghouse, a carved wooden stamp is used for a table; some glass beads are the lighting.

This hut features a netted hammock made from some rope ribbon. The 1.5-inch ukulele resting in the hammock is made from wood and hemp twine. The traditional Polynesian patterned rugs are hand-drawn on white fabric to give the appearance of a woven design.

Dragonfly Daycare

As a new grandmother, Nancy MacBride chose to create *Dragonfly Daycare* for Florence Griswold Museum's *Faerieville U.S.A.* With the exception of the ceramic stump, the buildings are created from a mixture of natural materials, upcycled materials, Aves Apoxie®, and found objects.

Wee fairies enjoy a campus-like area surrounded by the woven wicker sides of the vintage bassinet that Nancy slept in as a baby. This protective wall surrounds several buildings, a playground, and a craft area. On either side of the pathway outside the wall is a rose garden.

The hand-built ceramic stump has a toy room inside for rainy days. Including the vines, it is almost 4 feet tall. Its interior mushroom lamp creates a warm glow. On the "roof" of the stump, you might witness young fairies spinning and darting as they learn to fly and create aerial dances.

The orange Aves Apoxie® door has a circular mica window and opens into the first-floor foyer of the dining building. An earring finding is employed for the door pull. Upcycled wooden curtain rings are used for fairy swings.

Opposite page
These impressive double doors with dragonfly door handles lead into the dining room, where many snacks have been served. Surrounded by polished stones, the doors really open—much to the delight of children.

Dragonfly Daycare emphasizes the arts for young fairies' creative growth with painting and weaving stations.

Birch-Bark Light-Up Fairy Houses

Carol Betsinger created these whimsical light-up fairy houses from sections of hollowed birch logs found on the forest floor. As the wood of the fallen tree rots, the beautiful outer birch-bark shell remains intact. When you are creating fairy houses, look for these treasures in the woods.

The birch bark is cut to size and sealed inside and outside with Mod Podge® Outdoor. The colorful framed windows and door are made of polymer clay, distressed with antiquing medium, baked, and sealed with satin polymer sealant.

These houses have solar fairy lights by incorporating plastic cork fairy lights made for wine bottles into a copper fitting that serves as the chimney of the house. Solar units can also be mounted on the back of the house near a back window. The lights are strung throughout the inside of the house. The lights can be turned on or off by a switch on the side of the plastic cork-like unit. The light glows through the cutout windows of these charming fairy houses. They can be used as outdoor fairy houses in the garden or as indoor night lights.

The Grand Hotel

Made by John Curtis Crawford, this rest-and-rejuvenation site is for fairies from all over the realm. It is a gracious, cozy hotel in a lovely meadow surrounded by woods, with a river singing its way through the scene. In the evening, when the fireflies come out and the harps and flutes begin their song, the fairies recount the events of the day over succulent fruits and aged wine while the stars send sparkling dust to celebrate the occasion.

This hotel is constructed from cedar root from the Eastern Cascades, Oregon, and agate from the Sonoran Desert in California, along with jade, lapidary scraps, and blended sand.

Toast and Tea Tavern

Andrea Riggillo-Masia believes that the fairy community needed a tavern for the love of tea, B&Bs, and Britain's fairies.

Photographs courtesy of Caryn McCowan

The 18-inch-high tavern is constructed with oak bark and a wattle-and-daub exterior.

There is a natural acorn tower, and the roof lifts to a guest room.

In the rear is the Honey Bee Company. The chimney is a recycled paint tube covered in stucco and stone with recycled wood pieces.

Light House and Village

Steve Rodger's fairy house village was featured as an exhibit at Connecticut's Beardsley Zoo in its historic Victorian greenhouse. Steve focuses on reuse and recycle for his fairy houses!

Photographs courtesy of Jack Bradley Connecticut's Beardsley Zoo

A green aloe drink bottle was the structural element for the Fairy Power Tower. Birch and maple sticks frame the windows and walls. Steve applied a lightweight concrete product to the bottle with Popsicle sticks. Before attaching the tower to the other parts of the building and diorama, he added lighting. The shorter round tower was created using a gallon spring water jug. Using the same lightweight concrete material, he placed pea pebbles into the concrete before it dried. To create the roof, he built a basic cardboard geometrical structure and then masked it with birch bark and other natural materials. The entrance center structure started its life as a square plastic peanut jar.

This is the top of the tower on the 3-foot-high Fairy Power Tower. This butterfly has a second life as a resident of this fairy village. She's probably waiting for her fairy friends to show up for tea.

Ladybug Lodge

Photographs courtesy of Tammi Flynn

Madeline Kwasniewski knows that fairies love flowers, insects, and birds. The letter *L* in the alphabet is the theme for her fairy lodge. *Ladybug Lodge* is on Lavender Lane with lavender trees, a lavender path, and lavender ladders.

Ladybug Lodge is 12 by 24 inches. Its six small ladybug tenants, Lovely Lily, Lucy, Lisa, Lynn, Leslie, and Liz, are made from dried rhododendron leaves painted bright red with black polka-dot geranium leaves. The L-shaped driftwood is decorated with wire latticework.

Inset: The arbor and door of *Ladybug Lodge* are made from driftwood. Lavender-painted stones are laid down as a pathway accenting the lavender weeds used as a background.

The little ladybugs, Lovely Lily, Lucy, Lisa, and Lynn, like to climb on the L-shaped driftwood.

Family Tree House

Mark Clark designed a multilevel expandable house, using wood and other materials he has found in the woods.

This house is tiny: the main living quarters are 2.5 inches wide, the front deck on the second floor is 1 inch wide, and all doors measure 0.75 inches high. The base of the tree house is cypress; each floor is a cypress tree limb with a piece of oak slab in between. The overhanging roof is made from oak twigs with beechwood bark and moss.

The pathway is composed of crushed recycled concrete and lined with rocks. The well house to the right is constructed from twigs and has a grapevine bark roof. The ground cover is a mixture of different-colored sawdust. The front door is made from pine.

Left: This night view of the house highlights the third-floor balcony.

Sugar Plum Fairy Bakery

Jessica Zeedyk's *Sugar Plum Fairy Bakery* was part of the 2017 Wee Faerie Village at the Florence Griswold Museum.

The bakery sat on three tiers of tree slices. This tier shows the kitchen atop a wood slice measuring 18 inches in diameter. The fairy bakery features a shell basin sink, a driftwood baker's rack, and copper wood-fire oven. Preparations are underway: ingredients are ready; batters are being mixed; cookies are being cut out; and a blueberry tart is baking in the copper oven.

Right: Café seating is on the left of the bakery's selling floor. The tables are made from wood slices and some laser-cut wood discs found in the scrapbooking section of the local craft store. You can see a fairy has just been enjoying a slice of cake and some tea at one of the bistro tables.

Top: The bakery's awning-style roof is made from coconut fiber liners for potted plants. The tarts, cakes, and cookies are displayed on the wooden display rack. A combination of nail polish enamels and Mod Podge® is used to make their jelly fillings and sugary glazes.

Inset: Made from polymer clay, the breads, muffins, and scones are on display on a 5-inch wooden shelf. Once the polymer treats are baked, Jess uses a dry paintbrush over chalk pastels to give the breads a "crust" finish. The color is sealed with a polymer clay matte-finished glaze.

Left: The polymer clay pies are just a little larger than a penny (0.75 inches in diameter). A dry brush chalk pastel was used on these pies. The berries were a mixture of polymer clay; a glossy polymer clay glaze gave them their wet look.

Tiger Lily

Madeline Kwasniewski has lovely tiger lilies growing in her garden. She immediately thought of Tiger Lily, the princess in the story of Peter Pan, and she built a village.

A Native American headdress encompasses the fairy-sized Native American village. The headdress size is 3 feet wide by 5 feet tall. The ten stiffened-fabric tepees have singed edges with painted designs on the exterior. Rope ladders abound because the fairies love to cling and climb about. Madeline's signature fox is hiding under a blanket near one of the tepees. *Photograph courtesy of Tammi Flynn*

The seventy-three headdress feathers are made from cedar branches; they are sliced thin, bent, and notched to flow like real feathers. The decorative beadwork is cut tiny twigs; the trim consists of 406 willow branches, each cut at 90 degrees.

The tepees form a circle. The drum that Peter Pan and Tiger Lily danced on is made from wood and stretched and stiffened cloth.

Cottages at the Sea

Jayne Argus and Leigh Squires created this village inhabited by gypsy fairies.

You can see a basketful of berries that have just been picked in preparation for a night of dancing ahead. Pink sea glass makes a circle around the gypsy fairies' crystal ball, which is composed of a shell and a rose quartz sphere. The fairies will definitely take this with them when they continue their travels. Shiny blue glitter can be seen on the sand, where the fairies have danced previous nights. What fun and magic!

But when they abandon the village, how very sad.

Enchanted Irish Fairy Village

Jessica Marro's client wanted a fairy village with an Irish flair to celebrate her family's heritage. Jessica constructed the village with natural materials that she collected during her long walks at the beach, in the woods, in nearby parks, and on trails. Welcome to the *Enchanted Irish Fairy Village*!

Wouldn't you want to live in this enchanted village with the fairies? Tucked into the hillside, the village has everything you will ever need, including quaint bungalows for your family and friends. As you arrive, you can make a wish at the local wishing well (Dean Mian) before you go up the hill, where you can stay at the Leprechaun Inn or hang out in Shenanigans Irish Pub. You can go to your local bank (Ar n-Adh) and shop at O'Mailley's General Store. When it's time to worship, you can do so in the tiny chapel. You will always be welcome here. Love, joy, and peace are everywhere.

The fairies work hard gathering materials to make their village beautiful while hiking in their local area or when traveling. Each little house is made with love and tells a story as unique as its owners. The fairies use shells and beautiful sea glass from their seaside trips, glass beads representing their favorite colors, and found silver charms that help bring sparkle and uniqueness. Local moss, tree bark, twigs . . . whatever they can find that is natural. As you can see from this aerial view, each rooftop is different!

Right: This charming house belongs to one of the local residents. She loves butterflies, the color green, and spending time in her garden with her grandchildren.

The O'Mailley family members were the original founders of this Irish village. They live happily on top of the hill in their own private neighborhood. Jonathan and Sherry have their own abode where everyone feels welcome. Their door is always open; they hold the key to the village. Their children, Paisley and Judson, live nearby. The houses are interconnected by meandering wooden steps.

Mallie and Daisy are the local dogs. The two dogs greet everyone with their wagging tails and make sure everyone finds their way and feels safe. They love dog bones and the little silver charm over their door is just a gentle reminder.

The Leprechaun Inn is on the second floor of this building; all fairies are welcomed. They must know that the music and sounds coming from the pub will keep them up late, but that is just fine with them.

Shenanigans Irish Pub is the place to be. The fairies receive the best Irish food and drinks. Local talent will be singing and dancing at all times of the day and night.

O'Mailley's General Store is the oldest building in the village. Recently renovated, it was Jonathan and Sherry's original house. It has the same seashell details as their new home. Whatever you need, from fishing tackle to school supplies, you will find there.

The tree bark used for the exterior walls came from local trees; the moss and rocks used for the edging are from the same area. Green beads are scattered throughout, because green is the fairies' favorite color.

The Chapel

The tiny chapel is the newest and the tallest structure in the village. Faith is important for the villagers. It also holds the local schoolhouse. The bell rings every hour on the hour—a beautiful sound indeed.

Colony

Christopher Frost found the perfect location for his fairy homes. He built a small colony for the fairies in a group of trees. He completed the biggest structure with his daughter, Basil.

Located on a major bike path in Massachusetts, this fairy colony is a cluster of domiciles, walkways, and ladders in the sky. Some of the buildings are reflective of architectural styles—Gothic, medieval, mission, classic New England—but the majority are simply fantasy. It is made from wood and painted.

This fairy colony has gone through four stages. Annexes were added to different clusters of trees.

Fairies can walk or fly between the different buildings. An aerial boardwalk is a fun way to view the scenery.

— 2 —

Cottages

THE PICTURESQUE FAIRY COTTAGES FEATURED HERE ARE BRIGHT WITH WHIMSY. SOME ARE MEANT TO SURPRISE FOREST HIKERS OR TO DELIGHT THOSE WHO WANDER THROUGH THE GARDEN; OTHERS ARE MEANT AS TABLE DECOR. THEIR FLARED BARK SIDING, HAND-HEWN TRIM, IRREGULAR CHIMNEYS, AND INTRICATE DOOR KNOCKERS ARE PROOF THAT SOME OF US STILL BELIEVE. ALL HAVE IRRESISTIBLE CHARM!

Old MacDonald

Mark Gabrenya of Lexington Community Farm in Massachusetts created this amazing fairy farm inspired by the stone cottages that are common in the Cotswolds region of England.

The farm is situated on a raised accessible garden bed planted with various vegetables, including Swiss chard, thyme, rosemary, and lettuce seedlings. A terra-cotta pot became the duck pond. Birch branches created the cottage structure, which was then paved with river stones and colorful glass. The roof is moss. Willow branches were woven into a wattle fence and trellis.

Half a plastic water bottle was fashioned into a greenhouse.

Bottom left: A terra-cotta pot turned on its side became a barn for the goats. A cardboard tube became the inner support for the water well.

Twig and Moss Home

A good starting list of fairy home building materials includes colorful stones, small rocks, pebbles, seashells, pine cones (big and tiny), twisty twigs, bits of bark, dried leaves, lichen, moss, acorns, shelf fungus, acorn caps, chestnuts, dried grasses, feathers, and pussy willow catkins (the fuzzy part).

Julie Garvin Riggs built this simple fairy house by using three sticks of similar length and using them to form a tepee. She used twine to wrap the sticks together where they touch, and then tied the two ends of the string together. She added two sticks that are just a bit longer than the distance between two of the legs. These became the bottoms of the two sidewalls, which she secured with more twine. By using sticks with fungus and lichen, she enhanced the final form. Once the structure was built and secure, she decorated it with more natural elements, using her glue gun.

Fairy Alchemy

John Curtis Crawford was the architect of this house, while his collaborator Bridget Wolfe wove together stories whispered by winds and fairy wings for John's creations.

Fairy Maya inherited this mystery house from her grandfather, who had been its keeper for longer than anyone could remember but who had finally gotten tired of the job and taken off to the South Pacific to tend mango trees. No one else in the family wanted to go near it, but Maya had always been fascinated by the intricate alchemy of the house and her grandfather's lifelong search to master its flow. When Maya was young, her wings were barely strong enough to carry her, but then her grandfather taught her the theory of the house: that when you put the right objects in the right order in the chalices that surround the house, the magic will speed around the pathways and jump the chasm between the upper and lower worlds. When the energy leaps across, it spans dimensions and lands in the realm of magical laws, which allow the creation of anything one can imagine.

This house was constructed from sycamore from the Cleveland National Forest in Southern California and Bali greenstone from Indonesia. The sand is a mystical blend.

69

Woodland Fairy House

Abigail Stout creates tiny houses to enchant those fairies who live in the woods and those of us who walk in the woods!

A warm welcome awaits all fairies who come across this little woodland house.

Crystal Cave

Fairies know the delight in finding and collecting shells after a high tide or in coming across small sea creatures in those small tide pools. They know that the most soothing sound in the world is the lapping of waves—and that no smell is better than the salty sea air.

Often the homes contain natural crystals, precious stones, and gems—such as these amethyst crystals and rose quartz—to entice the fairies to call these caves home!

Jayne Argus and Leigh Squires make fairy homes to attract fairies in the natural alcoves on the sides of mountains or small rocky areas near the sea.

Uldred the Gnome

"Gnomes are fairies too," says Andrea Riggillo-Masia.

This house is just 6 inches tall, covered in moss and oak bark. An empty paint tube covered with tiny stones is the chimney. Behind the door is a handmade alcove bed, and the handmade table is set for dinner. *Courtesy of Caryn McCowan*

Oroville Log Cabin

Photographs courtesy of Katrina McCaul / @moseymeadow

Built by Pamela Godsoe, this little log cabin started with a pine house structure that was adorned with sticks cut to be log siding.

A scrap piece of pine became a door with a mushroom overhang. The doorknob is a jewelry finding. The pine boards used on the roof were burned with a torch, sanded, and protected with a coat of clear, water-based poly. This process highlights the beautiful wood grain of the boards.

Inset: Sticks were used to create the acorn-festooned window casings and moldings. The chimney is a piece of wood covered with birch bark. Preserved moss is tucked in around gaps and the chimney.

Fairy Tent

The creation of this 9-inch fairy tent by Jayne Argus and Leigh Squires began with searching for the perfect piece of bark that was strong and curled with a little opening for the entrance. They used bark from a mango tree.

Jayne and Leigh know that fairies are attracted to shiny objects, so they decorated the inside with sparkly stickers or foil for a shimmering glow. They used a strong base (wood or thick cardboard works best) and glued the bark upright onto the board base. Some extra bark made a tiny chair, table, and steps for the entrance. Some avocado leaves with sewn (or glued) tips together made the roof. Bougainvillea flowers sit atop the tent. They come in some of the spring fairies' favorite colors and can last for weeks.

Birch-Bark Play House

Carol Betsinger created this birch-bark house to inspire hours of creative play for children.

The roof is made from curly willow and red dogwood branches. Wisteria vines are woven in and out of the branches to form the partial bedroom walls. In the backyard is a stone fire pit that has a flickering light formed from a battery-powered votive candle.

Forest Tree Fairy House

Forest tree fairies love houses in the trees with their feathered friends. This unique fairy home is styled like a bird's nest. Jayne Argus and Leigh Squires made this home by twining and twisting twigs together over a basic woven bird feeder.

A neatly woven miniature basket is hung ready to be used to gather berries and nuts.

Inset: The roof was covered in bark from gum trees and sprinkled with a light dusting of dried flowers and dried grass clippings, tiny twigs, and leaves. A naturally bent branch provides a little landing perch for a forest fairy to explore this new abode.

Fairy House Builder's Cottage

Andrea Riggillo-Masia decided to build a house that she would live in—if
she were a fairy.

*Photographs courtesy of
Caryn McCowan*

She built the cottage from wood and used stucco and stone
on the exterior with a moss-covered roof.

A carpentry table with tools sits inside.

A house-shaped tea strainer was recycled into a mailbox.

Berkeley Rustic Woodland Cabin

Pamela Godsoe's cabin started with building a base structure from pine boards.

All photos are courtesy of Katrina McCaul / @moseymeadow

She decorated the structure with mini clapboards and made a ladder to access the upstairs apartment. Pine cone scales shingle the roof. A mushroom is the upstairs entrance roof. An interesting stick tops this roof to create the interest that fairies appreciate.

The window panes are crushed-glass "Diamond Dust" glitter. The chimney is a repurposed plastic piece that has been heated, bent, and applied to the roof. Ash bark is used as corner molding. The siding is a forest green that melds with its surroundings, which pleases the fairies.

Fairy Cottage Journal

Mare Faulds included a fairy cottage cover on a blank journal.

Using fabric and mixed-media opalescent and pearl mediums, Mare formed this enchanting cottage—complete with a front door.

Small botanicals, faux leaves and flowers, and miniature mushrooms adorn the woodland scene.

A removable tree fairy is situated just inside the door, housed in a sculpted, three-dimensional, oval spot.

Miniature Fairy Cottage

Diane Lilly's vision for this miniature house was one of whimsy and fairy tales. She wanted something that reaches for the sky with pinnacles reminiscent of Gothic arches.

For a short period of time, the fairy got to live in the herb garden in the backyard. So many little places to play and hide!

Diane began considering how this house would integrate into her herb garden. She added some Spanish moss to the top to make it blend in better.

Diane drew and hand-cut the main portions of her fairy house from planks of basswood.

She added a chimney, painted the house with craft paints, and glued river rocks around the doors and windows and in patches around the house to mimic the look of an old house that had lost some of its stonework.

Above: Here it is, nestled on a terra-cotta plate with faux succulents, a resin swing, river rocks, and moss.

Left: During the Christmas holidays, Diane covered the terra-cotta plate with white fabric, then added faux winter decor and fairy lights inside and out to bring a festive sparkle to this Christmas-themed fairy house!

Gourd House

Tori Stevens's inspiration comes from the natural world and exploring its aspects. Here, she takes a gooseneck gourd and works her magic with it.

This quad-level house is compact yet spacious at the same time, with everything the modern fairy needs. It stands about 22 inches tall. The home features a main-level great room with a bedroom and dining area; the other levels lead to the bathroom, the chicken run, and the observatory on the very top.

On the first deck, these fairies have a unique Colorado aspen toilet located right under the stars—just how they like it. Extra toilet paper and a broom sit nearby.

Inset: At the top of this magical place lies the observatory. Fairies don't care much about time in the way we humans think about it, but they do usually keep track of the length of days for gardening.

The handmade fairy bed uses sticks, clay flowers, and acorns and is accented by a painted sunburst on the headboard. The glowing fireplace and the acorn top sconces all are built using micro-LEDs.

Fairies usually just fly up to different levels, but their guests may need ladders. The stick ladders curve along the sides of the gourd, providing access to the many levels. Clay lanterns light the way.

Three cantilevered decks are attached to the gourd house. The top functions as an observatory and wild bird habitat, the middle level is where the chickens and bunnies live, and the lowest level is where the toilet is conveniently located nearest to the indoor living area. The decks are supported by sticks, acorns, and lots of hot glue. The railings are made from the seeds found within the gourd.

Forest Fairy Home

Kathleen Nolan believes that this is the home of an elite tribe of fairies.

This 8-by-10-inch folk fairy home has an earth fairy on its
door. The fairy has a genuine peridot in its forehead. It is
made from clay, an antique key, nature pieces, living moss,
and rocks.

Ashwood Workshop

Any fireplace log can become a naturalistic fairy house according to Pamela Godsoe.

Take your log and add some moss-covered bark and pine cones to make a roof. Mosaic glass pieces create windows. Sticks create window and doorframes. A wooden bead completes the door.
Courtesy of Katrina McCaul / @moseymeadow

House in the Woods

Created by John Curtis Crawford with the story by Bridget Wolfe, this cabin holds the key to your memories of what it is to be a fairy.

You could wander down every wooded trail, follow each winding stream, or track a squirrel, a blue jay, or even a white rabbit with a pocket watch and still never find the old ruin where a fairy statue stands atop a mound of weathered wood and stones. But if you're one of the humans with a touch of fairy blood, then you'll follow music that only you can hear, until you find yourself at the edge of a shimmering glade, where trees in soft moss dresses and coats wrap their arms around the ancient fairy shrine.

Pine Cone Fairy Cottage

The fairies love their flowers, and this cottage built by Tori and Kevin Stevens has them growing everywhere! Even the pine cone thatch roof has bright flower faces peeking out from among the sticks, bark, and branches.

The walkway and front garden, as well as the interior corners of the cottage, all feature high-mountain forest pine cone seeds painstakingly glued in place one by one. The scale is 1:12 (1" = 1'). The cottage is about 18 inches wide by 13 inches deep. The handmade log bed and side table were made by Linda Kozik, Rustic Miniatures. Tori decorated the bed with flowers, moss, and glitter.

The fairy cottage is open to all manner of wildlife that might wander by. On this occasion, we spied the two bunnies who keep their own little cottage out on the porch, along with some birds nesting nearby. The cottage windows feature handmade curtains with stick rods, and they're finished with painted trim, a bark window box, and fairy dust. The chair partially seen in the photo was also made by Linda Kozik, Rustic Miniatures.

The MOOnie Home

MOOnie the MOOcher, an Instagram cow-about-town influencer, commissioned a fairy house, now lovingly known as the MOOnie Home, from Jessica Marro. MOOnie's design wishes were simple: she wanted a fairy house that was cozy for her to snuggle in with her beefy curves and that could also travel across the universe with her.

This fairy architect is always looking for ways in which to repurpose bits and pieces of Mother Nature into her imaginative designs. She constructed the MOOnie Home with organic materials that she collected during her long walks at the beach, in the woods, and in nearby parks.

The two-story MOOnie Home includes a front porch, where MOOnie often hosts visits from fairy guests, as well as a few of her traveling animal friends. All who set eyes on the MOOnie Home entrance feel welcomed and charmed by its wondrous design, including the fireplace with logs to keep MOOnie and her guest fairies warm and toasty and the hammock in which to spend evenings relaxing and pondering the meaning of life.

The MOOnie Home is a hit among fairy visitors because of its many delightful features, including a wire bicycle with button wheels—where MOOnie does her morning workout. What more could an influencer cow wish for?

Starry Night

This fairy house by Sinia James asks you to use your imagination, call on your fairy friends, and enjoy a cup of tea while searching the skies and stars.

This house is made with weathered, recycled woods, including old painted shelves, branches from plum and birch trees, several various mosses, mini pine cones, preserved juniper, and artificial fern.

The second floor has a telescope for stargazing.

The Turtle

Many mythologies explain that the world is carried or was created on the back of a turtle. Nancy MacBride envisioned a fantastic fairy tower on top of a slow-moving turtle.

*Photographs courtesy of
Lauren Correa*

What is under THAT turtle? Well, Nancy heard, "It is turtles all the way down."

The medium-sized turtle is encircled by a wreath of golden deer antlers, from which sprout a color wheel of mushrooms. Each mushroom is a sanctum for fairies to settle in and meditate on the natural world around them.

The smallest turtle crowns a shining glass tower, from which he watches for fairies that need rest and relaxation in the turtle tower.

Inset: Lace, beads, and incised textures decorate the structure. The "skin" of the structure is Aves Apoxie®.

Can you find the big, medium, and small turtles? The largest turtle creates a sturdy foundation for this fairy tower. His extra-tall shell holds overnight accommodations for weary fairies. He smiles broadly as he moves slowly through the forest. Sometimes a ladybug, toad, or praying mantis will hitch a leisurely ride.

The mushrooms are created from plastic cups and bowls. They have tiny lights inside for when the fairies are in residence. The (removable) top tower was created with a battery-operated lantern. The largest turtle's shell is an aluminum turkey pan and a small plastic trash basket. His sturdy legs are PVC pipe. The height of the tower is 50 inches. The length from turtle nose to tip of tail is 26 inches. The diameter of the mushroom circle is 24 inches.

Fairy Houses

COTTAGES ARE TYPICALLY SMALLER, WITH A DISTINCT CHARM AND COZINESS; HOUSES, ON THE OTHER HAND, TEND TO BE MORE SPACIOUS AND PRACTICAL, CATERING TO THE NEEDS OF A GROWING FAMILY. THEY OFTEN FEATURE MODERN AMENITIES AND CAN BE FOUND IN A WIDE RANGE OF LOCATIONS, INCLUDING SUBURBAN AND URBAN AREAS.

24 Buttercup Row

Jill Dolan works intuitively with the fairies guiding her.

Photographs courtesy of Heather Varner of Five Feathers Photography

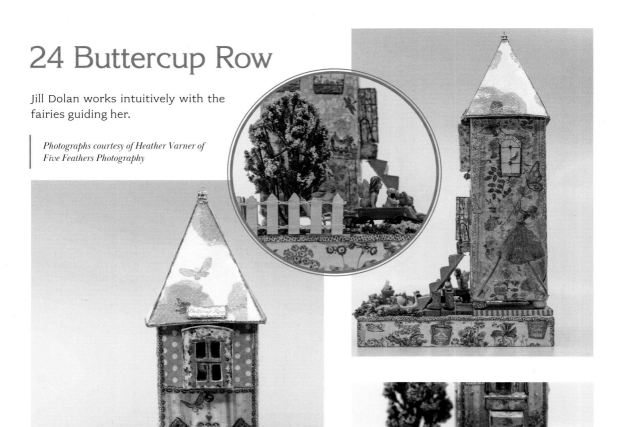

A welcoming fairy stands at the front door of 24 Buttercup Row. Outside, another fairy enjoys sunning herself while dipping her toes in the sparkling duck pond.

This house is crafted from a variety of materials: a milk carton, papier-mâché, dried flowers, acrylic paint, collage, embellishments, recyclables, glitter, various miniatures, and, of course, fairies.

Inset: A side view of the house highlights the plants and flowers decorating the yard.

Another fairy and her dog sit in her Radio Fairy Flyer while a forest squirrel and a calico cat converse with Deirdre the Duck, who floats happily in her ducky pond. A red-breasted robin has flown down from the Crann (a fairy tree) and is perched on the fence, singing a magical tune as she watches everyone have fun.

Anniversary WeeFolk Home

Pamela Godsoe created a fairy house for a unique anniversary gift by using a log from the wood stove pile.

Pam carved a heart out of the bark and wood-burned the couple's first names in the heart on the back of the house. The address is their last name, with the house number being the month and day of their wedding. She stacked and adhered sticks for the roof and chimney. Pam created the door and windows by carving into the thick bark of this ash log and painted them with acrylic paint. She used a glass bead as the doorknob and attached a square glass bead as a window to the door. She also made a wind chime using bells.
Courtesy of Katrina McCaul / @moseymeadow

Tranquility House

This house began as a project for one of Steve Rodgers's customers, but it became very personal. He ended up making a different house for that customer and keeping this house in his fairy barn when it is not on public display.

The Peace Window uses nature's recycled gift, sea glass.

Steve made this chimney (as well as chimneys on other projects) from an old beer tap handle from his venue-owning days. Hot glue and superglue affixed pea pebbles to the wooden tap handle's base. Small clamshells made perfect birdbaths, and empty acorn housings and quartz crystals became exterior fairy lights.

Fall Oak Fairy House

According to fairy lore, oak trees are sacred and are considered a storehouse of great wisdom. Carol Betsinger observes that bringing oak into the house or garden is a way to enhance contact with the fairy realm. Finding a fallen hollowed oak in the forest is a sad sight, but this tree offered itself to a new life of beauty and possibilities with Carol. That is how this once-beautiful tree was reborn into a fairy house.

This fairy house majestically stands 28 inches tall and celebrates autumn.

The house has two levels: a kitchen and a bedroom. The ceilings of these rooms light up with battery-powered fairy lights, which illuminate the crystals (to which fairies have a strong attraction) hanging from the ceiling of each room. The floors are paved in pebbles that have been grouted and sealed. This opening from the bedroom leads to a porch supported with gnarly "oak" trees with colorful silk fall leaves. A whitewashed wooden swing hangs below on one of the branches.

Inset: The roof is shingled with California white pine scales. Colorful silk fall oak leaves and acorns adorn the peak of the roof at the base of the copper chimney.

The first-floor kitchen has a crystal light. On the other side of the house is a rope ladder that leads to a lookout point on a tree fungus.

Maple Leaf Lane Toad Abode

Pamela Godsoe reminds us that toads are beautiful creatures to invite into the garden. Preparing a toad home in a shady part of your garden will help keep you pest-free as well as create a magical spot for the fairies to play.

Photographs courtesy of Katrina McCaul / @moseymeadow

Pam says, "Start by finding a cool, shady spot in your garden or yard: under shrubbery would be a good start. Toads need damp, dark, and cool temperatures to survive and to stay hydrated."

Be sure the area is free of herbicides, pesticides, chemical fertilizer, and trash. Toads breathe and absorb water through their skin. This makes them very susceptible to toxins.

"Toad homes should not have a bottom/floor; toads need to burrow," Pam explains. "The home should have at least one opening. Make sure the opening/entrance is the proper size for the native species in your area. You should not use cedar boards/wood. Cedar oil is an irritant to toads' skin, as are oil-based paints/sealants."

"Once the area is cleaned, prep the soil by 'fluffing' the top 4 to 5 inches of the soil with a garden trowel/fork," Pam instructs. "Toads burrow into the soil to stay hydrated and cool, and for protection against predators. Once the soil is fluffed, set your house over this spot and push it down into the soil slightly. Adding a handful of dried leaves or grass inside will also benefit your new tenant."

Pam continues, "Next, add a water feature, which can be as simple as a shallow dish buried in the soil and filled with fresh water. Be sure to add stones to the bottom of the dish for footing and to prevent drowning. Keep the dish full and the water fresh."

Maple Leaf Lane Toad Abode was created with pieces of scrap boards. The fabric leaf shingles were applied to a board by using wood glue and protected with a clear, water-based polyacrylic. Pea stones were adhered to a scrap piece of wood for a chimney. Scraps of driftwood created molding around the roof, door, and windows. Sticks and mosaic mirror pieces completed the windows; a glass bauble was applied to create the door window. Metal hinges and a glass bead are the finishing touches to the door.

Home Sweet Home

There are many levels to the fairy mansion made by Tori and Kevin Stevens! The little people love animals, and the main floor features habitats for fish as well as bunnies. The middle and upper levels are home to birds, plus all manner of critters who occupy a garden. The house is in 1:12 dollhouse scale.

Photographs courtesy of Kevin Stevens

The mansion features aspen columns, along with wood and river rock siding. Clay flowers encircle the columns and reach up toward the stick balcony railing.

The rooftop garden is accessed from the second level by using the stick ladder; candles light the way. This is where the gardening tools are stored, along with the garden hose. The custom-made upstairs door to the master suite has a tiny crystal doorknob.

The master suite was created using a dormer with two operable windows that invite summer breezes.

The fireplace is made from wood, river rock, and hand-painted lights in the firebox. A tiny friend of the fairies resides on the mantel—a hamster!

The little people snack on wine and cheese by candlelight while cooking dinner at the fireplace. Copper cookware and utensils are favored; they're lightweight and easy to fashion.

The fairy mansion's sleeping quarters feature a stick-made bed, a bookshelf lit with candles, and a real acorn lamp. The en suite bath includes a fairy toilet fashioned from high-mountain aspen, plus a mirror, a cup, and toothbrushes.

Fairies are known travelers, and they have everything needed here for cozy homelife as well as for planning the next adventure. The dining area displays freshly baked bread on the table. A well-stocked pantry in the back contains canned and dry goods.

The rooftop garden sits atop the master suite, and this is where the fairies cultivate flowers, fruits, and vegetables. Candles rest on the stick fence to help illuminate the weeding and watering tasks done by moonlight.

The fairies have been busy growing the most gorgeous veggies this season, and the bunnies and birds have been busy eating them! There's enough for everyone in this magical place.

Coastal Fairy House

Mark Clark wastes nothing. When you look at his projects, you realize how much he uses from nature.

This fairy house is made with a cypress base, driftwood, grapevine, oak, pine, moss, glass, seashells, acorns, and other assorted found objects. It is approximately 11.5 inches tall by 13 inches wide.

Inset, opposite page: The living quarters have an acorn-topped railing. The blue light is made from sea glass.

Clockwise, from top left
The upper level of the oak tree living quarters has a side ladder entrance to the pool area. Note the handrail.

The coastal courtyard has a multilevel patio deck made from pine, with a moss carpet over the base with recessed deck steps and a hand-carved door.

The comfy seating made from bark, seashells, and acorns is movable.

Alpine Fairy House

Fairy garden artist Abigail Stout instructs us how to build a house from wood.

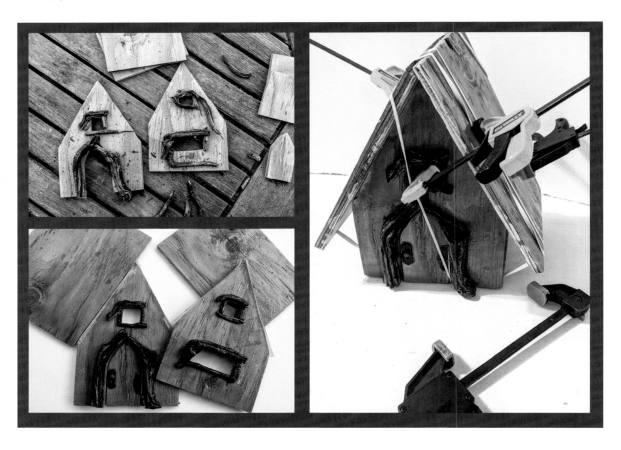

Start by designing your house on paper. Draw and measure your walls, front, back, and roof. Cut these pieces of paper out and make sure they all fit together before cutting your wood.

Once your house has been cut, sand each piece. Now you are ready to frame your windows and doors. Find unique, twisted pieces of wood and cut them to fit on each window and doorframe.

If you have a functioning door, be sure to attach the hardware now. With the door hung and the frames measured, sand each branch piece flat and glue them to your base wood. Tape the sides of your house pieces so they stay dry. You are now ready to varnish the faces of your house pieces. Do not get any varnish on the sides, so that they will glue together properly later.

Once your varnish has completely dried, you can begin gluing your house together. Start by gluing the front, back, and side walls together to form a square box. Once that has completely dried, you can add the roof. You will need clamps for all of your gluing processes. The roof especially requires extra care. Use as many clamps as necessary. Rubber bands also work.

When your house structure is complete and dry, you can add an additional top branch along the roofline of the house. This branch adds a decorative touch as well as protects the house from rain entering the top. Finish with any additional natural materials such as pine cones, seeds, acorn caps, or shells. Add a final layer of varnish to keep it protected from the elements.

— 4 —

Castles, Chalets, and Other Serendipitous Structures

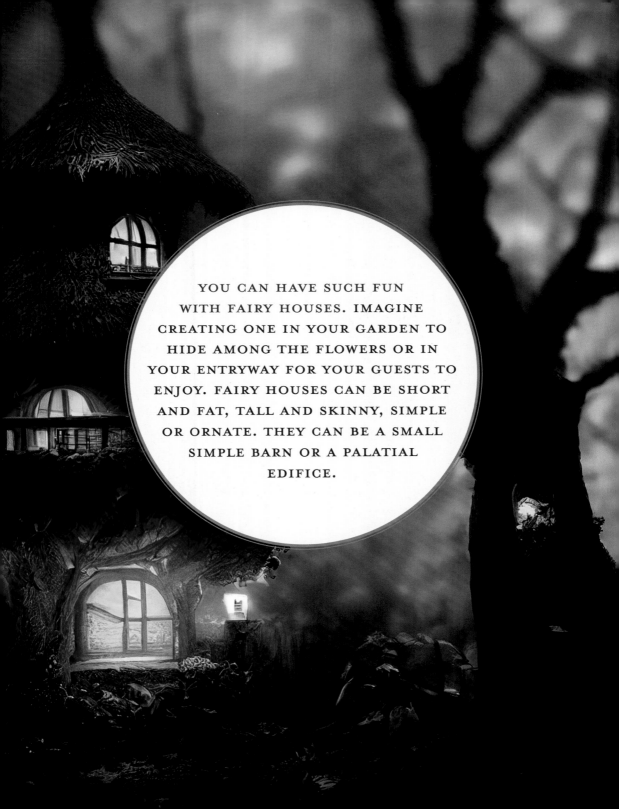

YOU CAN HAVE SUCH FUN
WITH FAIRY HOUSES. IMAGINE
CREATING ONE IN YOUR GARDEN TO
HIDE AMONG THE FLOWERS OR IN
YOUR ENTRYWAY FOR YOUR GUESTS TO
ENJOY. FAIRY HOUSES CAN BE SHORT
AND FAT, TALL AND SKINNY, SIMPLE
OR ORNATE. THEY CAN BE A SMALL
SIMPLE BARN OR A PALATIAL
EDIFICE.

Fairy Castle Journal

Mare Faulds points out that fairies have royalty too! Deep in the woodlands of the forest is an enchanted castle nestled in the trunk of a tree.

A fairy carriage sits outside, awaiting the princess who is just inside the drawbridge entry.

To create an enchanting royal design for her journal, Mare uses fabric, leaves, foliage, fantasy film, and opalescent mediums.

Inset: One of the two handmade fairies is nestled inside a small cove sculpted in the faux tree trunk on the back cover of the journal.

Honoring the Witches of Salem, Massachusetts

Photographs courtesy of Caryn McCowan

Twigs and potions, pumpkins and dragons . . . Salem, Massachusetts, is known as the witch city because of the 1692 Witch Trials, which claimed the lives of over twenty innocent victims.

Andrea Riggillo-Masia made the witch hat roof from recycled costume samples sewn together patch-like with a cardboard base, and she used rough-grade sandpaper for roof shingles. The foundations are stucco and stone foundations.

Left to right
On one wall is a hearth and mantle.

The structure is well decorated.

The window opens to dinner on the table.

Tiki Fairy Island Paradise

Before Steve Rodgers begins work on a commissioned fairy house project, he always has an in-depth conversation with the customer to learn about their interests and personality. The customer for this house wanted it as a gift for his wife on Valentine's Day. During the conversation, Steve learned that some of her interests and sentimental thoughts included an affinity for "tiki stuff" and the number 22.

The tiki fairy island house is built on a 12-by-18-inch sturdy Masonite base. The roof is preserved floral grass, which was affixed one layer at a time to a bark roof, using more hair spray than a 1980s prom dance! Lighting was installed later.

Steve drew a tiki-style face onto balsa wood and then carefully carved it with hobby blades. He painted it with acrylic paint, added a matte seal coat on top, and secured it to small pieces of driftwood

Mermaids at 999 Sand Dune Bay

Photographs courtesy of Caryn McCowan

Andrea Riggillo-Masia lives near the Atlantic Ocean, where she looks on the beach for shells and driftwood for her fairy houses.

This fairy house is made of recycled wood and covered with six layers of sand. A mermaid lives within.

Shells, seaweed, sea glass, and a mermaid adorn this house.

111

Fairy Glamping Tent

"Nothing is better than a little bit of 'glamping' with your woodland fairy friends," says Sinia James. "This tent takes me right back to playing in my backyard, making 'houses' with sticks, leaves, and mud. As a 'grown-up,' I can now create what I visualized as a child."

The tent is made with plum tree branches, preserved juniper, pine cones, moss, wood scraps, and faux fur. Inside the tent are pillows and sleeping bags made with various cotton lace and denim floral fabrics.

The working fire pit is made with small rocks, moss, plum tree sticks, a metal hook with an acorn pot, and a battery-operated "fire." The chairs around the fire pit are made with vintage millinery leaves, wood scraps, and seashells.

Inset: To add a little whimsy, Sinia made a pom-pom banner that attaches to the top of the tent and to a juniper branch. The height of the tent is approximately 14 inches, the length is 9 inches, and the width is 8 inches. This fairy house took approximately two weeks to complete.

The Tin Man's House

Madeline Kwasniewski was inspired by *The Wizard of Oz* when she made this 9-by-18-inch house.

The roof shingles are made from hand-cut aluminum flashing, cut twigs are used for the siding and wood stacks, and the windows and door are made from Popsicle sticks. The path is painted yellow to symbolize the Yellow Brick Road. The Tin Man's tin coat and pants dry in the breeze on the clotheslines made of twigs. Red glitter is used for the Tin Man's heart, located in a steel wool bird's nest. An antique oil can and other articles are scattered about the yard.

Thumbelina's Kingdom

Do you remember Thumbelina's story? Nancy MacBride does.

In the foreground is Thumbelina's bedroom and foyer.

Thumbelina's dining-room tower looks over the "mirror" pond.

Food deliveries are left in the foyer near a portrait of Thumbelina's friend, the swallow, who rescued her from marrying the mole. The long ladder is for guests lacking wings, while the fairies can land on the two balconies.

The beetle on this gourd is a reminder of the insect, frog, and vole who tried to marry Thumbelina. Thankfully, she managed to get away from those terrible suitors. This gourd has a remote-controlled, battery-operated flickering tea light.

In the interior of the dining room, the floor is a plate with morpho butterfly wings under glass. Milkweed pod chairs are pulled up to the table. The base boasts freshwater pearls.

Inset: This view of the dining room reveals the larder cabinet. All windows really open and close. The copper trim on the dome should patina beautifully.

Breast Cancer Awareness Hollow

As a cancer survivor, Mark Clark was honored to help the fairies make this hollow out of driftwood.

One end of the driftwood appears to hug a visitor in a protective embrace; the other end is a sheltering cave of exploration. The area in between allows for rest and relaxation; it's hoped that any worries will drift away. Meanwhile, a visitor can draw strength while sitting under the awareness symbol with friends and family.

In the illuminated hollow at night, the infinity pool, which is great for sunbathing in the day, becomes a glowing gem. The lighted patio lets all visitors enjoy the fresh air and night sky without being in the dark.

The functioning well house is made from bark, twigs, and moss. The lower door to the living quarters also leads to the hollow. The upper level is a cypress tower topped with grapevine bark.

The Mistress of Time

The celestial realm above, the spirits of earth and nature, and the four directions of the compass all are woven into the web of time in John Curtis Crawford's and Bridget Wolfe's collaboration. Reassured that the beat goes on, the Mistress of Time settles down on the bench for her daily meditation. As the hands of time stroll past the symbols, new stories unfold in her vision. She is always excited to see what time will bring today.

All the "numbers" are runes with specific meaning for the owner of the clock to contemplate whenever he or she has time. For example, the time shown on the clock is *Othila*, which has to do with separation, shedding old skins, and *Inguz*, which embodies the completion of new beginnings. The rune on the pendulum, which speaks to every time, carries *Dagaz*, which embodies a complete transformation.

The Windmaster

The Windmaster is one in a series of "tower" type houses by John Curtis Crawford. These structures invariably look like they are smiling and happy, a wonderful thing for fairy houses.

The house is made from stones, driftwood, and urethane resin. The windmill is wood with brass fittings, and it really moves in the wind.

A Flutter in Time

Vanessa Bunnell modeled this castle to represent stone castles in Loch Ness, Scotland, in the eighteenth century.

This castle is approximately 12 by 8 inches. Pine is used for its base construction, and stone and mortar create the layers. Acorn cap steps allow the fairies to climb to the top of the castle and then fly away.

Bless This Barn

Jessica Marro created this barn for her daughter Kaitlin, who loves her horses, Secret and Sox, with all her heart.

The bark used for the exterior walls and overhang was found nearby.

The water troughs outside each stall are made of acorns. The colorful beads represent the beauty and joy embodied in these horses.

Fairy Ferris Wheel

The fairies love Nancy MacBride's Ferris wheel because they can rest their wings and still fly through the sky while enjoying the music of the bells attached to the wheel. The capsules are colorful sculpted birds and nests festooned with charms, beads, and other surprises. Every capsule is a different color of the rainbow. Which would you choose to ride in?

The wheels are Hula-Hoops textured with hot glue and painted with coarse pumice acrylic and acrylic paint. A gigantic metal bolt through an antique industrial spool constitutes the axle. It has nuts on the end of the bolt, with fabric flowers covering them. The spokes are salvaged from a library card catalog. Bells are attached to the spokes, and they ring as they glide down the spoke when the wheel is turned. Flat stock metal legs are attached to wooden "feet" from an old armoire. The "feet" are bolted to a base that—in a previous life— was the top of a dresser!

The birds and nests swing freely from wooden dowels that create strength inside heavy-duty plastic straws. Large beads attached to the bottom of plastic champagne glasses were slipped onto the straws. They hold wire that, in turn, holds the birds, which were crafted from yogurt cups and cut plastic milk jugs.

Each nest took several hours to make. Real moss and plants were woven into a rattan cup shape. Stitching with waxed linen reinforces the natural elements and incorporates beads, charms, and sparkly items into the nests.

— 5 —

Fairy Accessories

FAIRY DWELLINGS CAN CONTAIN
MANY DIFFERENT ACCESSORIES—EVEN
THE FAIRIES THEMSELVES!

Bridge Fey

Nancy MacBride channeled her love of nature, spirituality, and objects when she designed Fey. Fey "lives" on a hemlock tree beside a footpath through Voluntown Peace Trust in Voluntown, Connecticut. She has three smaller figures, companions, or babies on other smaller trunks coming out of the same tree. Fey greets hikers after they cross a footbridge over a stream.

Top left: Fey began as a 32-ounce yogurt cup, bubble wrap, and a long wooden bead through which wire was threaded for her arms. Layers of tape and papier-mâché created form. Using Aves Apoxie®, Nancy finished the sculpting, added texture, ensured strength, and waterproofed. She then cut a smaller hemlock tree coming out of a cluster of exposed roots to about 5 feet high, and screwed the torso into place on the cut trunk. Acrylic paint, bark, leaves, and vines helped Fey become one with the tree. Glass eyes gave her face some life.

Top right: Bridge Fey is participatory in the way that people might put a garland of flowers around a statue of the Virgin Mary or bring offerings to a statue of Buddha. People often leave offerings. One passerby left Fey a clamshell that is glued shut; perhaps it hides a written secret or a wish. Another hiker gifted Fey with a beautiful amethyst stone. During a storm, a branch fell and damaged Fey's arms. Nancy reattached Fey's arms so that instead of reaching overhead, they are more secure in a cradling position to hold offerings. Fey has changed very little over the ten winters that she has watched over hikers.

Inset & bottom right: The caretaker of the property lovingly dresses Fey and her "babies" for winter with fabric shawls and branches of pine.

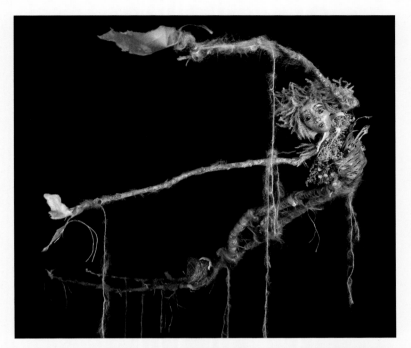

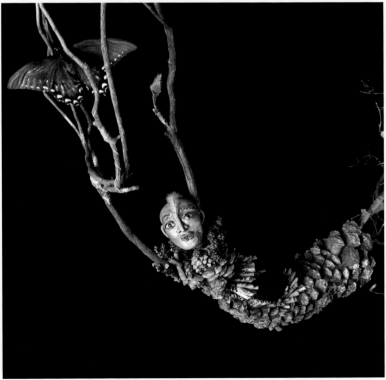

Nancy also made two sprites to bring magic into our lives.

Furniture

Tori and Kevin Stevens work together. Kevin works with wood and makes custom wooden furniture for regular humans in addition to the fairy folk. For their projects featured here, Kevin did the traditional woodworking and assembled the wooden houses, while Tori created the design, decorations, and stick furniture.

Saturday night at the cabin—all is warm and cozy as the hedgehog family enjoys a quiet evening around the wood stove in their forest log cabin. The bed and rocking chair were purchased as unfinished dollhouse furniture and then decorated using paint, moss, acorns, and fairy dust. The wood stove is an altered vintage toy stove that was cut open and wired with tiny LED lights. The switch is on the bottom of the stove. *Hedgehogs courtesy of Julie Rodgers (@TheFlossInn on Instagram)*

Here is a table-side view of how closely our feathered friends live with the fairy folk. This dining set provides a safe place to raise baby birds, and their birdsong strengthens fairy magic. Win-win! It is built using aspen wood.

Thick moss blankets the silk flower ferns to create the softest, sweetest dreamtime for fairies.

Several slats and lots of hot glue were used to make sure the bed was strong enough for baby fairies to jump on it! Moss and fairy dust conceal the glue, and silken ferns cover and secure the foundation.

Doors

A small door hidden in the woods or your garden leads to a place of magic. Fairy house designers pay a great deal of attention to their doors because they know what is on the other side.

Nancy MacBride created a door surrounded by polished stones and her signature "cheerios" doughnut forms that leads to a fairy nap room.

Kathleen Nolan used nature pieces, clay, an antique key, and artificial flowers. Any type of fairy or forest folk may be hiding out behind this door! It is 12 inches tall by 10 inches long by 3 inches deep.

Pixie Portal

Created by Jessica Zeedyk, this magical entryway sits on the grounds of a sculptor's studio.

The door measures 10 inches high and 5.5 inches across and is affixed using furniture tacks to the trunk of an eastern red cedar tree. The main medium for the doors and window frames is polymer clay in various faux finishes: stone, copper, gold, and obsidian.

The windows are made from scraps of stained glass, mounted on glow-in-the-dark polymer clay. It gives the appearance of a warm glow emanating from the windows as the sun starts to set. The entryway is dressed for fall, using polymer clay pumpkins and moss, dried grass, and dried hop buds.

Inset: The intricate sunshiny face of the door knocker is made from a metallic-finish polymer clay. This door knocker probably has something to say as a fairy approaches. Its face measures 0.75 inches in diameter.

A dash of color and found objects enhance any door.

Magical Fairy Portal

Pamela Godsoe tells us that having your own fairy portal is possible even if you don't have a garden or tree. A magical door can be made with minimal supplies that you may already have on hand. By setting up a door, you're welcoming the fairies into your home.

Photographs courtesy of Katrina McCaul / @moseymeadow

Scraps of cedar adorn this door. Wooden shower rings were used to create portal windows. Wood slices of various fallen tree branches were used for steps. Bark was attached to the roof for shingles, with preserved mosses tucked in here and there. Jewelry findings and old hinges were repurposed to decorate. Some of the fairies move to warmer climates during the winter, but this home's residents stay year-round.

While residing in New Mexico, Pam made this door with a scrap piece of pine board. She sanded down the corners to add a curve and hand-carved grooves into the board, to create the illusion of individual boards. Sticks create the door molding. Pieces of jewelry findings, a mini drawer handle, and twigs found on the forest floor added the perfect finishing touches to complete this project.

Flower Portals

Abigail Stout makes delightful tulip fairy doors.

Tulip doors are hand-painted with a gradation of color, starting with white at the bottom and slowly expressing beautiful spring colors as the tulip unfurls at the top. Doors open by hand from the center petal. They are best used at the base of a tree or wall, where they can add color and a delightful fairy entrance!

Carved Doors

Krista Silver hides some of her doors.

These magical fairy doors hidden in your garden can lead to fairies' other worlds. Made with wood and moss and some special magic to make the doors' windows glow at night, they let you know the fairies are safe and warm inside.

Swings

Jayne Argus and Leigh Squires designed several special swings. There could be fairies in your garden! Have you ever noticed a delicate gossamer thread (an abandoned spider's silk) dangling from a tree branch? If you find one of these swings and it's still swaying back and forth, your garden fairy may have seen you coming and disappeared in the twinkling of an eye, since fairies are very wary of humans.

Left to right
Golden leaf, found naturally, is twisted into a fairy swing. So beautiful only nature could create it.

A curled gum tree leaf makes the perfect swing. It drifts effortlessly through the air until it finds its place among gossamer threads in the most hidden places.

A sturdy fairy swing was made from a small piece of bark from a huge gum tree, perhaps for the enchanted folk or gnomes to use.

Bottom right: Designer Krista Silver made a swing with wood, moss, and some pretty little flowers. A ladybug keeps watch.

Stairs

If you have a tree trunk, you can make a set of stairs and a door as Jayne Argus and Leigh Squires did here.

Australian bush fairies usually make their homes in tree trucks. This one is over 5 feet tall. Although fairies can fly, they sometimes take the steps to rest their wings, or have a stairway so their small bush animal friends can visit. There are eighteen wooden cookie spiral stairs.

A small log and rope ladder, made easily from fallen sticks and twine, can be lifted up or left down for little visitors and easy access. The hidden door was made by framing a natural curve in the tree truck with bark. A tiny wooden mushroom clearly defines the doorknob.

Fairy Sign Project

Abigail Stout knows youngsters love to make things, and a sign is a perfect way to get them interested in the garden.

You can use a purchased board, a found board, or even some plywood, as long as it has been sanded smooth with 400-grit sandpaper. The size should be large enough for a child to work with comfortably. The sign shown here is 5 by 8 inches. Next, gather some acrylic paints and soft paintbrushes. Have your child start on the edges with dark-green paint. Using a tapping motion, create a dotted green background on the sides. You can use several shades of green or a single shade, depending on the child's age and painting ability.

Then add some pinks and tall flowers. These would resemble hollyhocks. Have the child start at the bottom with a full brush of paint. Work upward into smaller blooms toward the top. You can help your child do this by holding their hand and tapping the brush lightly on some sample paper first and then letting them do the sign. Repeat this flower type in purple. Next, you can fill in with some small dots of red. These would be berries that grow along the bottom of your child's garden on this sign. So, keep these dots very small and round with a tiny paintbrush. All these paint strokes are done by dabbing, so even a very young child could do this project with help.

Use several coats of polyurethane on both sides of the sign. Be sure to include the string when you polyurethane the sign. The polyurethane on the rope will help it hold up to the outside elements. Your young friend will love to care for the garden with this cheery sign showing the way!

Fairy Ponds

What fairy doesn't want a cool pond to soak her feet in or to take a swim and cool off after a long day in the hot sun?

Krista Silver's fairy ponds are made with fresh river "water" and stones, and she adds some flowers and moss to make them pretty. Some of them have magical glowing crystals and glowing "water." A little glitter makes them sparkle!

Other Accessories

Krista Silver makes her magical potion tables with wood, moss, glowing potions, and handmade miniature books. This charming little magic table makes a perfect addition to a fairy garden with books, moss, and a pink crystal.

Left: Krista added a mystical fairy-gazing ball sitting on its own little stand in a little spot with flowers and moss, a magical wand, and a magic-item page.

Right: Abigail Stout makes sure that the fairies receive their mail. She used fine sandpaper on a disc piece of wood. She glued a flat stone, a flat wood branch (top and bottom), and the wood disk together. Then she cut a small plastic cylinder (an old candy container or film tube) in half. She hot-glued a corn husk to one half of the cylinder. The covered half cylinder was then glued to the top of the wood disc, and the entire piece was decorated with moss, flowers, and leaves.

— 6 —

The Designers

OUR DESIGNERS CERTAINLY KNOW
FAIRIES AND THEIR WORLD. SOME OF
THEM WERE IN OUR EARLIER BOOK;
OTHERS HAD AN EXCITING NEW
APPROACH TO THE WORLD OF FAIRIES.

Jayne Argus and Leigh Squires

Who says magic doesn't exist? At Garden Sparkle in Australia, every day is magical because Jayne and Leigh can help make fairy garden dreams come true for people all around the world. Leigh's construction knowledge is perfect for helping to create whimsical complex designs, and Jayne is passionate about the enchanted world of fairies. Fairies and fairy gardening have been a part of Jayne's life for as long as she can remember. It began when she was blessed with a mother whose imagination and kindness created the most magical world a child could ever dream of, including her contribution in helping create these beautiful fairy homes seen in this book.

Leigh and Jayne know that believing in fairies is also about caring for our beautiful world and the animals who inhabit it with us. For every order, Garden Sparkle provides a meal for a rescued animal in need, so when you start creating your fairy homes and gardens, you are also helping their furry friends. They love to see the joy that fairy gardening brings to people's lives through all the photos and messages they receive.

Website: www.gardensparkle.com.au
Facebook: www.facebook.com/gardensparkle
Instagram: @gardensparkle

Carol Betsinger

Carol grew up as a child of nature, playing in the forest near her Illinois home. Fallen trees became her secret world; the beauty of the woods nourished her imagination. Her life was blessed with two beautiful daughters and five grandchildren. Her older daughter died at the age of thirty in 2007 from complications of cystic fibrosis. She had a passion for fairies, and one of her prized treasures was the first fairy house that Carol had ever seen. After her daughter's death, Carol combined her love for her daughter with her innate love of nature to create her own fairy houses.

Carol believes that fairy folklore has given her an understanding of the ways of the fairies.

She works to incorporate their whimsical spirit into each house she has built during the last decade. Each one is created with garden and expired woodland materials.

Etsy: www.etsy.com/shop/FaeryGrrlGardens

Vanessa Bunnell

Vanessa has participated in the Florence Griswold Museum's Wee Faerie Village since 2016. Her first project was for the theme "A Flutter in Time," and she chose a setting of eighteenth-century Scotland to incorporate her love of gardening. This project took several months to complete and included putting live Scotch cap moss plantings into broken pot pieces, collecting natural materials, and working with her children's local elementary school art program to make tiles for stepping-stones. She wanted to bring to life the color and texture of the Scottish Highlands by incorporating natural stonework in the castles and using live plantings.

This annual project has become a full family activity. Vanessa consults with her father, a retired carpenter, on structural design and durability; works with her mother, who collects any and all craft supplies; and involves her kids as much as they will let her. Working on fairy projects has given her an opportunity to create garden art with her family and community.

Website: smithsacres.com

Mark Clark

Growing up on a third-generation farm in the heart of the Adirondack Mountains, Mark became a fan of Winnie the Pooh and his many adventures. Now Mark owns FourAcreWoodsUS in North Carolina, where he can let his imagination come to life. Learning early on never to waste anything, he opted to pursue woodworking and foraging. Thanks to Mother Nature and hurricanes, there is an abundance and variety of wood to repurpose; he loves the challenge of making bespoke pieces from what nature provides.

During the pandemic, Mark decided to challenge his woodworking skills, which led to the creation of his first fairy house kit. He wanted to design something that adults and children of all ages and skill levels could use to create their own work. This led to his next fairy house, the Woodland Fairy Family Tree House, a multilevel expandable house limited only by imagination. He welcomes all to come stroll, hop, skip, jump, and fly through FourAcreWoodsUS and see where the paths—or lack thereof—lead you.

Website: FourAcreWoodsUS.com

John Curtis Crawford and Bridget Wolfe

John, who passed away in 2022, was a working professional in the arts-and-entertainment industry for more than fifty years. He designed and built magical creatures and miniature habitats for feature motion pictures, TV, and commercials. His lifelong passion for wood, stone, and wild, natural places kept him tuned to the voices of fairies and other elemental beings, who served as his muse in the creation of these magical houses.

To create his houses, John gathered materials carefully, collecting stones, sand, and twigs from mountains, desert, and sea. No living branches were ever cut; the twigs were all naturally shed. John looked for personality and energy, and he loved the shapes and character of natural things. He rarely went anywhere without a pair of pruning shears and a collapsible saw. When he found things that touched him, he felt driven to bring them together to form something, once explaining, "It feels almost like introducing friends that you think would like each other. I sometimes think of it like a dating service for twigs and stones." His passion was to give form to the many voices that speak to him through twigs and stones, and to let his sculptures tell stories of the wild places of the Otherworld.

Bridget is a teacher, writer, myth keeper, and storyteller who weaves stories whispered by winds and fairy wings into the fabric of everyday lives. Her relationship with the mystical world began in childhood, and she has spent more than forty years studying shamanism's maps of the Otherworld. She blended the teachings of medicine wheels and sacred ritual together with master's degrees in English and clinical psychology to create ceremonial retreats and rites of passage and has guided learning journeys to sacred sites in the Americas, England, and Ireland.

Bridget's forays into the Otherworld have found expression through her love of language, first as an oral storyteller and more recently as a writer of mystical tales. She believes that "we have to bring what we can imagine into reality." In her collaboration with John, she wrote fairy-tale vignettes for many of his fairy house sculptures and graphic images.

Website: www.fairywoodland.com
Facebook: www.facebook.com/FairyWoodland/
Twitter: @fairywolfe

Jill Dolan

Jill is a self-taught painter and mixed-media artist who uses collage, journaling, embellishments, recycled materials, found objects, fairies, animals, painting, pen and ink, and more in her creations. She pays great attention to detail in crafting in her art.

As a child growing up in California, Jill was fascinated by small and found objects and would construct little houses and other creations out of the various bric-a-brac that she found. She has always viewed the world through a kaleidoscope of colors, texture, figures, and magic. Many of her creations center on community, embracing positive messages using colorful and joyful images to make places where everyone is welcome! Her art is for everyone to enjoy; children are especially drawn to it. She thinks of her creations as enchanted pieces that will inspire people by evoking positive remembrances of home, family, and location and encourage others to honor their own memories and the lives of loved ones, past and present. Most of all, she wants to make people happy and hopeful through her art, especially in dark times, because a little bit of magic can make big and wonderful things happen!

Facebook: www.facebook.com/jilldolanart/

Mare Faulds

Mare lives in a cottage-style home in northern Michigan, surrounded by woods that provide lots of inspiration for creating mixed-media handcrafted journals. She is especially fond of using recycled materials in her artwork along with fabric, paint, and vintage items.

Website: linktr.ee/lilacpages
Etsy: www.etsy.com/shop/LilacPages
YouTube Channel: Lilac Pages
Instagram: @Mare_LilacPages

Christopher Frost

Christopher is a sculptor living and working in Somerville, Massachusetts. His work has been exhibited and collected in museums and art institutions throughout the New England area. His indoor and outdoor sculptures are part of many private and corporate collections.

He began his education at Bates College in Lewiston, Maine, and then studied at Parsons School of Design, Paris, France. He received a master's degree from the School of the Museum of Fine Arts in Boston.

Website: Christopherfrost.org

Pamela Godsoe

Pam was fortunate enough to be her father's shadow and learn many important building skills from a master carpenter. Although she will never be able to build a full-scale home, she uses these skills on a smaller scale. Of course, she works closely with the Wee Ones to ensure her creations are Fae approved.

When she was a child, her father created a mini entrance and a postal mailbox for the character Uncle Wiggly. Pam still remembers the awe and excitement she felt in witnessing this small world. This was the beginning of her interest in the Wee homes and the mini magical world. She started with houses for the Wee Winged Folks (also known as birdhouses). As fairies became more popular, she began getting requests for more WeeFolk homes. Creating them is a form of meditation for her. Once a WeeFolk home has been relocated, she is happy, knowing that she has sent a bit of magic out into the world. Pam believes that magic happens each time a person smiles and feels joy. She believes that adults tap into their inner child when setting up a magic area for the fairies. Encouraging imagination with tactile projects can be very beneficial.

Etsy: www.etsy.com/shop/LaDeDahDesignsMaine

Sinia James

Sinia (pronounced "Seenya") is a mother of three and a grandmother of four. She loves to sew, garden, decorate, and "rejuvenate" furniture. When she chopped down a fifteen-year-old plum tree and saw its beautiful branches falling to the ground, she became inspired. Her granddaughter ended up with a four-story, 5-foot-tall fairy house (with all the "fixings"), and her grandson has a dragon lair. Thirty-plus fairy houses later, her living room no longer exists.

To Sinia, "wonky" is a wonderful thing! Nothing is perfect, nothing is measured, and no two of anything are the same. She encourages people to find something that sparks their "inner child" or their imagination—or just simply brings a little bit of magical silliness to their life, patio, or garden.

Etsy: www.etsy.com/shop/PlumTreeFaerie

Madeline Kwasniewski

Madeline's ideas for fairy villages come from her childhood love of games, movies, gardens, and nature. She is a multimedia artist who uses wood, metal, stone, fabric, paper, and paints to create fun, happy, and whimsical forms. A retired entrepreneur, she dedicates her time to lifelong interests in creativity and design and to bringing joy and happiness into people's lives. Since becoming involved with the Florence Griswold Museum's Wee Faerie Village events, Madeline works annually to see the enjoyment in the eyes of the visitors, young and old.

Lexington Community Farm

Lexington Community Farm (LexFarm) is a nonprofit certified organic farm in Lexington, Massachusetts. The farm grows a variety of organic vegetables on 5 acres of land. The farm is committed to increasing access to local produce for households of all income levels. LexFarm provides hands-on education to foster connections to farmland, farming, and each other, through workshops, education programming, a CSA, and volunteer opportunities. Vice president Mark Gabrenya designed the farm's fairy house.

Website: lexfarm.org

Diane M. Lilly

The owner/designer/artist of Di's Studio Designs, Diane found herself led astray by the fairies! As a child, she would imagine where these tiny beings would hide or sit or play. How did they go about their daily lives? What did they do for a living? How magical it all seemed! What a perfect escape on a quiet afternoon. As an adult, she never lost the wonder for small worlds, but her fascination leaned more toward the design of miniature houses. She attended college for interior design and is interested in design and architecture.

Website: disstudiodesigns.com
Instagram: @disstudiodesigns
Facebook: www.facebook.com/DisStudioDesigns/

Nancy MacBride

In junior high, Nancy participated in an early 1970s educational experiment that tasked students with being responsible for their own learning. Instead of doing the learning units, they read novels and drew house plans as well as people to live in the houses. Someone told her that architects have to "be good at math"—so, unfortunately, she gave up on becoming an architect at about twelve years old.

Her art is assembled from found objects, natural and man-made (shells, bones, driftwood, pieces of discarded furniture, worn household items), combined with materials such as clay, metals, Aves Apoxie®, beeswax, wire, paper, and fabrics. She uses symbolism while working with these materials and employs meditative, repetitive actions, such as painting patterns, stitching, or incising textures. The construction, especially joining techniques, often informs the design of her finished work. Nancy realizes now that making fairy houses is a combination of imagining her characters and not having to follow the rules of math while being the architect.

Website: nancy-macbride.squarespace.com
Instagram: @re.galia_by_nancymacbride
Etsy: www.etsy.com/shop/RegaliaByNancyMac

Jessica Marro

Jessica Marro has a love for architecture and design, passion for the outdoors and hiking, an unwavering belief in fairies, and joy in creating for others. She follows the philosophy "Dream the largest of dreams, find joy in the littlest detail."

Website: littlewondersnthings.com

Kathleen M. Nolan

Kathleen subscribes to Stephen Nachmanovitch's statement "The most powerful muse of all is our own inner child" and believes it is the imagination of the inner child in all of us that creates and loves magical works of art. Kathleen's fondest childhood memories are of her mom pointing out the beauty of forest trees, twinkling stars, season changes, and other natural phenomena. From this appreciation of the wonders of Earth, sprinkled with imaginations of magic and glitter, her forest folk, fairies, and whimsical pieces were born.

As a member of the Plymouth Center for the Arts in Plymouth, Massachusetts, she has sold her pieces in several stores along the waterfront and had two art shows at the Art Shoppe in Plymouth. Her paintings hang in the Plymouth Town Hall and the

Holmes Public Library Children's Room (Halifax, Massachusetts). She has won three fine-art awards from the Pembroke Arts Festival for her Forest Folk. Two of her largest fairy homes hung in the John Carver Inn and the Water Street Café during the Fairy Trail Event in Plymouth in 2019. In addition, Getty Images owns the rights to five of her nature photos. Her artistic flair never tires of dabbling in "wonder."

Etsy: www.etsy.com/shop/ForestFolkStore

The Original Art Party

The Original Art Party is a small group of creatives that has gathered every month or so since 2009 for a day of shared art collaborations. Its slogan is "Keep Dreaming and Keep Building." Its first foray into a fairy build came several years ago, inspired by the long-running Wee Faerie Village at the Florence Griswold Museum. After the group shared pictures of its art projects with several museum staff members, it was pleasantly surprised to receive an invitation to participate the following year. The members were even more surprised to have *Ariel's Aviary* chosen to represent all the fairy artists at the museum due to COVID-19 restrictions. (Editor's note: You see; good things happen when you believe in fairies!)

Organizing the group via Zoom was the biggest challenge. This group of creatives consisted of William and Ian Evertson, Teri and Flip Prestash, Cynthia and Roger Abraham, Nancy and Lance Crouch, and Nancy and Jed Dolde. The co-captains were William Evertson and Teri Prestash. The group shared ideas and sketches, focusing initially on the central theme. From there, each of the couples created individual builds to complement the aviary structure. Its builders outdid themselves with a forest hospital, museum, recycling center, post office, bandstand, vineyard, and community center, in addition to the main aviary.

David D. J. Rau

David says, "Over a decade ago, we stopped to visit friends in Portsmouth, New Hampshire, en route to a summer holiday in Maine. This charming seaside town hosts an annual fairy garden festival; sadly, we just missed it. However, the thrill and magic of it all still hung in the air. Our friends enthusiastically pointed out where fairy houses 'were,' only days prior. Their enthusiasm for the phantom event was palpable. They vigorously cajoled me to consider something similar for the Florence Griswold Museum in Old Lyme, Connecticut, where I work as the director of education. 'What does the FloGris have to do with fairies?' I thought silently but nodded vigorously. I most likely rolled my eyes.

"Needless to say," David continues, "my eyes returned to earth a few years later when I was desperate for a good idea to help the museum weather financial hardships of the 2008 recession. Wee Faeries to the rescue! Since that first year, I not only coordinate the yearly, monthlong event at the museum but eagerly participate as a creative artist. I plan my fairy installations for months before the actual building begins. I make sketches, watch YouTube tutorials, and take stock of my home studio, where I store bags of reindeer moss, jars of acorns, trays of shells, boxes of prickly seed pods and soft and furry catkins (pussy willow blooms), and, of course, bundles of twisted twigs."

Email: david@flogris.org
Instagram: @davidrau8

Andrea Riggillo-Masia

Our lives are not all sparkles and twinkles, but they can be, if you listen to your heart's calling of innate creativity. At age forty-eight, Andrea did just that. While managing a restaurant and enrolled in creative-writing classes, she began crafting birdhouses with a personal touch for family and friends. She was asked by an author friend to re-create her fairy storybook into 3-D. After Andrea built a magical tree house, her friend asked, "How about building woodland fairy homes?"

Like the fairies, Andrea borrows, recycles, and renews: a button, a bobble, an acorn and an earring, a penny, and an orange peel, all for Earth's healing. She custom-builds from wood and bark or reconstructs birdhouses. She has created fairy life in the shell of an old clock and a hanging Moroccan lamp and built fairy-size custom replicas of family homes or businesses. Meditating is key: before each project; she imagines the lives of fairies and researches Celtic and fairy lore—and magical ideas flow freely. Her fairy chambers are created for indoor enjoyment. The best compliment she can receive from a client is "I want to live in there!" Her goal is to spread joy, leaving a little sparkle of magic.

Website: www.fairieschamber.com

Facebook: www.facebook.com/TheFairiesChamber

Julie Garvin Riggs

Julie is a teaching artist and museum educator who comes from four generations of artists. After traveling to Europe and Mexico, she returned home to Connecticut to help with the family business. Fortuitously, she signed up for a children's-book-writing class at the Florence Griswold Museum in Old Lyme. She was in the process of putting together two children's books of her own when she met David Rau, the director of education (and now her boss), who hired her as an art educator. With only two weeks to go before the very first Wee Faerie Village, she hit the ground running . . . and her life and art became fully immersed in all things fairy!

Fast-forward more than a decade and the yearly pilgrimage made by thousands of visitors, swarming the grounds to view the annual magic that is Wee Faerie Village, still inspires her. Thousands of Girl Scouts, school groups, and adult groups have attended Julie's fairy-house-making classes at the museum. The structure and the medium are changed each year: clay, cloth, tepee, dried gourds, and twigs have been among the offerings.

Email: julie@flogris.org

Steve Rodgers

A lifelong professional musician, songwriter, and miniatures artist, Steve lives in the bustling suburbs of New Haven, Connecticut, with his wife of twenty years, Jesse (who is also an artist). He began building train sets and dollhouses professionally in his early twenties. He founded and directed two community-minded live music and arts venues in Connecticut and ran them for fifteen years.

When his tenure as a venue owner came to a close, Steve went through a season of self-reinvention and discovery. In the spring of 2018, he built his first fairy house, a Mother's Day present for his wife. She loved it, and pictures of it started circulating through their local home-school and church communities. Through the power of social media, Steve began getting commissions to make fairy houses for others. He has constructed a modular fairy house village, which has been on exhibit in various public venues such as Connecticut's Beardsley Zoo. Steve is most at peace when surrounded by wild birds, building fairy houses, or playing guitar in his backyard.

Website: stephenpeterrodgers.com

Krista Silver

Wee World Construction was born when a little piece of the yard wouldn't grow much. Krista and her husband removed several dead bushes and plants over a year's time because everything planted in that spot kept dying. They added soil, plant foods, and fertilizer to no avail. The spot, however, would get covered with moss and little clovers, as well as twigs and rocks. What better place for the fairies to thrive in? Krista asked her husband about creating a hidden fairy garden in this little abandoned area. He was all for it, because their grandkids would enjoy it too.

Krista wanted natural, rustic items but couldn't find what she was looking for. So she made the items herself: ponds, little homes, and accessories such as snails, mushrooms, and stepping-stones came easily. Abracadabra, she had a fairy garden oasis! Her fairy village started, she realized—with the fairies' help—that making items was fun, creative, and a wonderful artistic outlet. Now making fairy garden items, she can work from home and use natural items to build a beautiful Wee World for herself and others to enjoy.

Email: weeworld@contractor.net
Website: www.weeworldconstruction.com
Etsy: www.etsy.com/shop/WeeWorldConstruction

Tori and Kevin Stevens

Tori's inspiration comes from the natural world and exploring its magical aspects through hiking, art, writing, and spiritual studies. Kevin shares this inspiration through working with wood and making custom wooden furniture for regular humans in addition to the fairy folk. For their projects featured here, Kevin did the traditional woodworking and assembled the wooden houses, while Tori created the design, decorations, and stick furniture. They both live and work in the wilds of New Mexico at their enchanted ranch.

Blog: Torisaur.com
Etsy: www.etsy.com/shop/MoonTreeTrading

Abigail Stout

As a lifelong gardener, crafter, and artist, Abigail takes great joy in creating miniature displays. Fairy gardens are places where imagination can come to life, and she tries to make pieces that look like they have been built by the elves and sprites. Searching for the perfect material on a walk by her creek is one of her favorite activities! She has found that using branches, driftwood, stones, and mosses discovered while hiking or camping makes fairy gardening possible for everyone. Abigail began the *Sprouted Dreams Podcast* (formerly called the *Fairy Gardening Today Podcast*) to help others find or expand their skills and create memorable displays.

Abigail has dabbled in many art mediums over the years. Much of her experience in pottery is applicable to polymer clay. Currently, she uses lots of wood and is exploring the extensive possibilities of her scroll saw.

Website: www.sprouteddreams.com
Facebook: www.facebook.com/SproutedDreams/
Pinterest: www.pinterest.com/sprouteddreams/
Etsy: www.etsy.com/shop/SproutedDreams
Listen to the *Spouted Dreams Podcast* on your favorite podcast player!

Jessica Zeedyk

Jess's passion for fairy homes and gardens originates with a love of miniature worlds, fairies, and all things fantastical. She has always been the artistic type: creating, painting, taking photos, exploring graphic arts, and constructing miniatures. These hobbies, combined with a vivid imagination, have helped her become an avid craftsman of miniature fairy dwellings, gardens, and knickknacks.

When Jess creates fairy projects, she begins with something in mind—and often it morphs into something totally unexpected. Getting started is all about the found objects; they build upon each other and speak to one's imagination. Each project is an adventure; there are no rules in the world of fairies. She doesn't think about scale or skill; she simply uses her imagination and the things around her to inspire. Fortunately, nature provides fantastic vision, and everyday found objects spark innovation. Whether making a fairy dwelling, garden, wreath, or wand, Jess revels in creating whimsy and magic. She loves that fairy work allows her the opportunity to express her artistic talents in such a unique way.

Instagram: @weewingsandthings
Facebook: https://www.facebook.com/weewingsandthings/

Appendix

PLANTS FOR YOUR FAIRY GARDEN

Fairies love gardens. The color, smell, and appearance of plants can attract them. When designing a garden for your fairy house, look for plants that match its scale, such as creeping phlox, polka-dot plant, peperomia, wood sorrel, small-leaved ivies, dwarf mondo grass, club moss, dwarf ferns, succulents, and dwarf grasses. For fragrance and texture, try herbs such as creeping thyme, watercress, and any of the chocolate mint varieties (although they will need to be trimmed). You can harvest some of the herbs for cooking too! Dwarf plants and slow-growing plants are useful because they won't quickly overrun your fantasy landscape.

Plants can be used for so many things in the fairy world: flowers for dresses, hats, shoes, and even cups; leaves for plates, umbrellas, and hiding places; moss for carpets, bedding, and cushions—and some plants are "big" enough for fairy beds. Some fairies love the sunshine; others love the shade. Fairies used to love green the most; now they love pink, purple, and blue too.

What you can make from natural materials is almost as limitless as your imagination, especially if you make it in miniature. If you like the desert look, plant small succulents, cacti, and sedums, but obviously don't add a moisture-loving plant into that mix. Fairy gardens often appear in shady nooks, where their shy inhabitants can hide away. Sunny areas, however, are ideal for fairy garden beach or seaside themes. Use slow-growing cacti and play sand to make a shoreline. Stand a big conch shell on its pointed end and turn it into a beach house. If your house will be in the sun, incorporate plants that can take the sun.

The downside to using natural materials is that they often break down more quickly than manufactured items, so if your fairy house is outside during a harsh winter, it may not last. But that provides you an excuse to build a new dwelling.

When starting a fairy garden, there are so many choices from A (ageratum) to Z (zebra plant). To have a healthy fairy garden, you need to consider a few things before you start planting:

Where will it be located? Inside or outside? In the sun? In the shade? Part sun and shade?

Will it be in a container or part of the yard?

How big will it be?

Will the garden be seasonal or yearly? Do you want annuals or perennials?

How much color do you want?

Fairy garden by Tori Stevens. *Photograph courtesy of Kevin Stevens*

Here are some favorite fairy plants.

PERENNIALS FOR SHADE

Ajuga—'Chocolate Chip', 'Pink Lightning'
Baby tears
Bluebells—Virginia
Club moss
Columbine—dwarf
Dwarf ferns
Epimedium—'Lilafee', 'Rubrum Fairy Wings'
Erythronium—'Fawn Lily', 'Trout Lily', 'Dogtoothed Violet'
Ferns—'Japanese Painted', 'Maidenhair', 'Lemon Button', 'Boston', 'Lady', 'Crinkle', 'Silver Lace'
Fernleaf—'Bleeding Heart'
Foxglove
Heuchera—'Coral Bells'
Hosta—'Mighty Mouse', 'Munchkin Fire', 'Funny Mouse', 'Wonderful'

Iris cristata (dwarf crested iris)
Lambs' ear—'Silver Carpet'
Lamium—'Orchid Frost', 'Purple Dragon', 'White Nancy'
Lavender—dwarf
Lily of the valley
Lungwort—'Raspberry Splash'
Primrose—'Cowslip', 'Blue Bellflower'
Tiarella (foam flower)
Trillium
Viola—'Heartthrob'
Vinca—'Bowles Periwinkle' (Thumbelina's sister is Periwinkle!)
Watercress
Wood sorrel

PERENNIALS FOR SUN

Artemisia—'Silver Mound'
Armeria maritima—'Sea Thrift', 'Cliff Rose', 'Lady's Cushion', 'Lady's Pincushion', 'Marsh Daisy', 'Sea Grass'
Bachelor buttons (cornflower)
Campanula (bellflower)—'Birch Hybrid', 'Dickson's Gold'
Creeping phlox
Dwarf lady fern
Dwarf mondo grass
Fairy rose
Geranium (cranesbill)—'Ballerina', 'Hens & Chicks'
Irish moss
Ivy—dwarf, miniature

Lambs' ears—'Stachys Silky Fleece'
Laurentia
Mexican heather
Mint—'Chocolate', 'Variegated Pineapple', 'Peppermint', 'Mint Apple', 'Mint Pineapple'
Ornamental strawberry
Peperomia (radiator plant)
Rosemary
Scottish moss
Sedum (stonecrop)
Thyme—'Elfin Creeping', 'Wooly'
Veronica Aztec gold
Violet

Italicized plants are cultivars.

ANNUALS

Ageratum
Alyssum
Calibrachoa
Celosia
Coleus
Convolvulus—'Dwarf Morning Glory'
Cuphea (false heather, firecracker plant)
Fuchsia—'Penta Fuchsia Nectar Plant'
Gomphrena—'Buddy Purple', 'Globe Amaranth'
Hypoestes (polka-dot plant)
Lobelia

Marjoram
Mecardonia
Melampodium
Nasturtium
Nierembergia (cupflower)
Ornamental Pepper—'Calico', 'Chilly Chili'
Oxalis (shamrock plant)
Scaevola (fan flower, fairy fan flower, half flower)
Succulents—'String of Pearls', 'Zebra Plant', 'Ice Plant', 'Baby Jade', 'Blue Spruce', 'Little Gem'
Torenia (wishbone flower)